Who is the Real Jesus?

Uncovering the Truth

H. Dermot McDonald

Isaac Publishing

Who is the Real Jesus?

Published in the United States by
Isaac Publishing
6729 Curran Street
McLean VA 22101

Copyright © 2012 H. Dermot McDonald

All rights reserved. No part of this publication may be reproduced, stored in a retrieval system, or transmitted in any form or by any means, electronic, photocopy or recording without the prior written permission of the publisher, except in brief quotations in written reviews.

Unless otherwise stated, Scripture quotations are taken from the HOLY BIBLE, NEW INTERNATIONAL VERSION. Copyright © 1973, 1978, 1984 by International Bible Society. Used by permission of Hodder & Stoughton, a division of Hodder Headline Ltd. All rights reserved. "NIV" is a registered trademark of International Bible Society. UK trademark number 1448790.

Scripture quotations marked "NRSV" are taken from the New Revised Standard Version Bible: Anglicized Edition, copyright © 1989, 1995, Division of Christian Education of the National Council of the Churches of Christ in the United States of America. Used by permission. All rights reserved.

Library of Congress Control Number: 2012932548

ISBN: 978-0-9825218-8-5

Book design by Lee Lewis Walsh, Words Plus Design

Printed in the United States of America

Who is the Real Jesus?

Contents

Foreword by Patrick Sookhdeo 1
Introduction 3

The Human Reality: "What kind of man is this?"

1. The Fact of His Real Humanity 7
2. The Development of His True Humanity 17
3. The Challenge of His Perfect Humanity 27

The Divine Reality: "Who do people say the Son of Man is?"

4. The Truth as It Is Revealed 39
5. The Titles that Reveal Jesus 69

The Redeeming Reality: "How can you say, 'The Son of Man must be lifted up'?"

6. The Nature of Christ's Work 85
7. The Names of the Worker 95

The Exalted Reality: "'Did not the Messiah have to suffer these things and then enter his glory?'"

8. Jesus Christ ... Crowned with Glory 107

Bibliography 117
About the Author 121

Foreword
by Patrick Sookhdeo

"Who do you say I am?" This question was posed by the Lord Jesus Christ to His disciples part-way through His ministry, after they had heard His authoritative teaching and witnessed His mighty works. It called forth from Peter the first recorded confession by a human being of His identity as the Messiah, the Son of the living God (Matthew 16:16). And it is as important a question for His followers today as it was then.

The New Testament writers paint a series of rich portraits of Christ, which together make up a powerful and coherent picture of the Son of God, who is both fully God and fully human. But many people in our own day deny the truth of this. Atheists and agnostics claim that Jesus was just a good man, like many other human leaders and religious teachers. Adherents of non-Christian religions put other human beings or gods on the same or a higher level with Him, or they reject key Biblical statements about His deity and divine Sonship.

Islam does both of these things. It places many other prophets on a level with Jesus, and it elevates the prophet of Islam, Muhammad, to a vastly higher place. It also declares that Jesus was just a human being and not God; that someone else was crucified in His place; and that He did not rise from the dead.

If these claims were true, they would tear the very heart and soul out of the Christian faith. Only because Christ is the Word of God made flesh (John 1:1, 14), who was in the form of God but was made in human likeness (Philippians 2:6-7), can He reveal God perfectly to us and open for us the way back to Him. Any attack on the person of Christ is an attack on the integrity of Christianity itself. So it is important that Christians learn how to respond convincingly to alternative views, by trying to understand what the Bible has to say about our Lord.

H. Dermot McDonald was an outstanding scholar and teacher, who lectured for many years at London Bible College (now the London School of Theology). I had the privilege of sitting under his teaching when he was my lecturer in 1967-8. He was commended for "his uncompromising fidelity to Biblical truth", and in this compelling book he clearly presents the teaching of Scripture on the humanity and deity of Christ.

Dr McDonald first sets out the Biblical evidence for Jesus' human nature. He traces how it developed through our Lord's earthly life and explains its profound significance for us. Then he puts the case for Christ's deity and explores it using the some of the exalted titles that the Bible gives to Him. He also discusses the saving work of Christ and its relation to His person, and celebrates His enthronement at the right hand of God.

I am delighted to commend this new edition of such a robust and rigorous introduction to the person of Christ. It uncovers the truth about the real Jesus, and will help Christian readers to respond to other views of who He is. By God's grace, it will also help them to grow in knowledge of the Son of God, who is no less than God Himself, incarnate in human flesh.

Dr Patrick Sookhdeo
February 2012

Introduction

The following pages should be read as an introduction to the study of New Testament Christology (that is, the doctrine of the person of Christ). I was asked to produce a fairly easy book to give Christian readers a better understanding of the Saviour in whom they believe and hope. I have tried to remain faithful to this commission.

I have begun from the assumption that the data of the New Testament is to be taken at its face value. This includes the view that the Synoptic Gospels (Matthew, Mark and Luke) provide the historical basis for faith, that the Gospel of John proves the value of faith, and that the rest of the New Testament demonstrates to the eye of faith Christ's relationship to the fellowship of the Church and the needs of the world.

So I have not discussed the relationship between the so-called "historical Jesus" and the Christ whom the Church confesses; nor have I tried to separate the message or significance of Jesus from the Gospel presentations of Him. My reason for not engaging in a new "quest for the historical Jesus" is that the Jesus of the New Testament is the only Christ we can know, and it is this Christ who is the focus and definition of the Church's faith. So I have not taken sides among the theologians involved in these quests. This is not because I think that the issues they have raised are unimportant. It is rather because the Christ who can be known is the Christ of the whole New Testament.

Putting the point more simply, I am seeking to fulfil a more modest purpose, namely to give a thought-provoking presentation of Jesus as human and divine. I hope, though, that Christian preachers and teachers will find help here for their tasks. They may find some ideas in the outline and treatment of the subject that can be filled out for the blessing and benefit of those whom they instruct in "the truth as it is in Jesus". In this sense what follows may be seen as a sermon for preachers.

Rudolf Bultmann has stated, "The interpretation of the biblical writings is not subject to conditions different from those applying to all other kinds of literature." This is both true and false. It is true because we are dealing with literature, with what is written. But it is false if we see the New Testament as like all other kinds of literature in every way. According to the Preface of the New Revised Standard Version, "the Bible has been more than a historical document to be preserved or a classic of literature to be cherished and admired; it is recognized as the unique record of God's dealings with people over the ages. The Old Testament sets forth the call of a special people to enter into covenant relation with the God of justice and steadfast love and to bring God's law to the nations. The New Testament records the life and work of Jesus Christ, the one in whom 'the Word became flesh,' as well as describes the rise and spread of the early Christian Church. The Bible carries its full message, not to those who regard it simply as a noble literary heritage of the past or who wish to use it to enhance political purposes and advance otherwise desirable goals, but to all persons and communities who read it so that they may discern and understand what God is saying to them."

I hope that what follows will be useful to those who seek an answer to the question, "Who is this Jesus who is called Christ?"

THE HUMAN REALITY

"What kind of man is this?"

Chapter 1

The Fact of His Real Humanity

The Evidence of His Human Life

It was in the calm that followed the storm that Jesus had subdued with a word that history's most important question was posed by His astonished disciples: "What kind of man is this? Even the winds and the waves obey him!" (Matthew 8:27; cp. Mark 4:41; Luke 8:25). What kind of human is this? The tone of the question suggests that the disciples were becoming aware of something unique and inexplicable about this Jesus of Nazareth with whom they had thrown in their lot. He was beginning to impress upon them the fact that He was somehow set apart and unique. He had just slept on in the midst of a howling gale that had suddenly churned up the Sea of Galilee into a dangerous cauldron, and that had brought the sailors, expert fishermen though they were, near to disaster. Yet He was asleep as though he were indifferent to their concern and their safety, and not apparently in the least bothered about His own. When they woke Him, He quietened the raging sea with a word, and immediately they realised that one who had appeared indifferent was actually invincible. What kind of human is this?

Yet He had been sleeping; this is the important fact. For this makes clear to us that however unique and inexplicable He was, He was no ghost. However much He might be more than human, He was not less. He was quite literally and truly a human being. It is with this fact about Jesus that we must begin, with the evidence for it and the importance of it. We can look at the evidence for the human reality of Jesus with reference to His natural life and His moral and spiritual character. His ultimate being will be considered later.

There is no doubt that Jesus had a *body* as real as that of other people. True, there is no evidence that He suffered from illness. There was a certain physical robustness about Him that allowed Him to make long journeys on foot and spend long nights in prayer. But are sickness and weakness necessary to genuine human existence? It is not obvious that they are. Like sin, they mark us all as being less than human, as being fallen humans.

Jesus was truly human, "being found in appearance as a man" in every way except those that make people less than human. He came into human life in the normal human way, by natural birth after a pregnancy of the usual length (Luke 2:6-7). He had a mother, as we all do (Galatians 4:4). He grew as other children do, to maturity and adulthood (Luke 2:40). He ate food (Luke 7:34-36; 14:1; 15:2; 24:41, 43) and knew what it was to be hungry (Matthew 21:18; Luke 4:2), thirsty (John 19:28) and tired (John 4:6ff.). He was limited to one place like other people, and so had to make His way from place to place. He suffered the indignity and inhumanity of a mock trial and a public execution (John 18:19-24, 28-33). The fact that His death was real and neither a temporary loss of consciousness, nor a faint, nor a sham, is unintentionally demonstrated by the Fourth Evangelist in his reference to water and blood coming from Jesus' side (John 19:34).

Jesus also possessed the *mental and emotional qualities* that distinguish humans from animals and make them more than just bodily. The Gospels clearly indicate that He had all the elements of a normal human personality.

Jesus displayed his normal mental processes by asking questions to gain information (Mark 9:21; Luke 2:46-47). He had clearly studied the Old Testament Scriptures and learned many passages by heart, as He showed during His temptations and throughout His ministry. His discourses, His questions and His answers also demonstrated the normal processes of thinking and reasoning.

He also displayed the emotions common to all people: the love of family (John 19:26), of friends (John 15:15) and of His own people (Matthew 23:37); and He could both feel love for strangers and receive it (Mark 10:21; 14:6). He could also express moral indignation (Mark 3:5; 10:14; Luke 11:46; John 8:44), was familiar with sorrow (Matthew 26:37, 38; John 11:33-36), could weep with distress or sympathy (Luke 19:41; John 11:35), and was moved with compassion many times (Matthew 9:36; 14:14; 15:32; 20:34; Mark 1:41; 6:34; 8:2 etc.).

It seems impossible to doubt, in light of Jesus' own words, that He had a will of His own (Matthew 26:39). His will was moved by various factors, like ours (John 7:1-10), and it acted in the same way as ours. There were occasions throughout His life when He had to steel His will against temptation and set His face towards the fulfilment of His vocation. The virtues of the will were particularly exemplified in the steadfastness and persistence with which He continued loyal to His calling despite the contrary suggestions of His friends (Matthew 16:22) and the consistent hostility of His enemies (Matthew 12:14; Mark 11:18).

Jesus' *spiritual and moral life* was also authentically human, though at the highest possible level of human experience. He knew God in an intimate and personal way. He was not one of the many who "seek after God", not even a successful one. He bore witness to God. His understanding of God was a prophetic testimony born out of His inner experience. His knowledge of God flowed naturally from His communion with God. He felt Himself always to be in the presence of God. He never had any doubt about God, because for Him God's presence was a living and felt certainty. He did not regard God as a hypothesis to account for the world, but as the Father who made the world.

Out of this living and felt awareness of God's reality and presence came Jesus' faith, prayer, joy and obedience in relation to God, and His service and patience in relation to others. His trust in God was real and wholehearted. He was not nervous or timid in the midst of life's uncertainties, because to Him everything was in the Father's hands (Matthew 10:29). It was this great certainty, this absolute confidence and trust in God, that accounted for His great courage and restfulness of spirit. He was neither anxious nor restless, because He knew that He was doing the Father's will.

Jesus sought places of solitude before His times of service. Even though He shared God's very life, He knew that He needed God. Even though He was sure of God all day, every day, He had to talk to God, to spend time with Him. He put into practice (Mark 1:35; 6:46) His own command to pray alone (Matthew 6:6). He prayed not just as an example to His disciples, as a model for them to copy. He prayed because He needed to pray, to find refuge in the shadow of the Almighty, to renew Himself with God's strength and find the courage to endure His ordeals through trust in His Father.

There is no fear in love, and the love of Jesus for God cast out all fear. Bound up with His love for and trust in God was the joy in God that was reflected in His words and actions. They reflected a mind-set of assured joyfulness. It was in this attitude of faith, prayer and joy that He fully obeyed the will of God. He had come to do the works of God, and having put His hand to the plough He did not look back. Jesus' spiritual life was thus *perfectly* human; it exemplified the standards that are required of all people, but that only He has met.

When we look at Jesus' moral life, we find all the virtues: honesty, compassion, patience and humility, and everything else that comes from a person's faith in God, fellowship with Him and obedience to Him. All that it means to be truly human is found in Jesus. In Him we encounter a real human being.

When we ask how important the humanity of Christ is to the Christian faith, we find that the Church has always sought to safeguard both its reality and its integrity. In its early days, in a context where the "spiritual" was believed to be more "real" than the "material", it was Christ's human nature (rather than His deity) that was most in doubt. The Church had to counter the Docetists, who questioned the reality of Christ's body, and the Laodicean bishop Apollinarius, who questioned its integrity. The Docetists thought it was illusory; the Apollinarians thought it was incomplete. The Christ of Apollinarius was neither fully human nor fully divine, but a "glorious mixture" of both. But an illusory or incomplete Jesus does not meet the requirements of the Gospel. The first letter of John was written (among other reasons) to show that the full humanity of Jesus is essential to the Christian faith (1 John 1:1; 4:2, 3), and the letter to the Hebrews shows that it is necessary for salvation (Hebrews 2:14ff.).

It is this fundamental Gospel truth of the reality and integrity of Christ's humanity that gives reality and integrity to the incarnation. However we interpret the incarnation, it is essential to note that it does not involve any diminishing of Christ's humanity. The Word became *flesh*, really and literally. In the person of Jesus Christ, the Word who was eternally with the Father took upon Himself a fully human life, entering into every aspect of human existence: physical, mental and spiritual. In the human Jesus "all the fullness of the Deity lives in *bodily* form" (Colossians 2:9). So the claim that Christ went the whole way is central to the Christian faith: "Since the children have flesh and blood, he too shared in their humanity" (Hebrews 2:14). To redeem us God has to share in our common human experiences, and He has done so in the real human life of Jesus.

For human beings and our salvation the reality and integrity of Jesus' humanity is of vital importance. Only someone who is truly human can act before God on behalf of humans. It is as He became one of us, obeying God, experiencing conflict and suffering death as a true human being, that He fully entered our human experience and was able to receive the divine judgment on human sin on our behalf. In Him divine grace became human, because He is fully human. Gregory of Nazianzus, the fourth-century church leader, challenged the incomplete view of Christ's humanity advanced by Apollinarius with the claim that any part of human nature that God has not taken upon Himself is not saved. Only if just half of Adam had fallen would Christ have taken and saved just half of our human nature; but since the whole of Adam fell, the whole of his human nature must be united to the whole of Christ's divine nature so that it can be saved as a whole. Gregory suggests that the Apollinarians are begrudging humans their full salvation by making Christ only a picture of humanity and not the reality.

So the declaration in John's Gospel that judgment has been committed to the Son of Man (John 5:22) is profoundly significant. Sinners need to know that their Judge can identify with them because the Judge has the same nature as they do. Only when the Judge knows both the persistence and depth of sin on the one hand, and the weakness and temptations of humans on the other, will the sinner be assured that the forgiveness that is offered is really for him. For believers God's goodness is proved by His great act of self-humbling in becoming flesh.

The Beginning of His Human Life

The story of Jesus' birth is told with great tenderness. It is not artificial, so as to detract from the "naturalness" of the event, but bears the mark of authenticity. The circumstances are stated only in so far as they point to the essential fact that a child was born to Mary. To the mother and those who visited the birthplace, there was no uncertainty; a real and new human life had appeared in the world. Despite the statement of the famous carol that "little Lord

Jesus, no crying He makes", we can be sure that everything that is essential to a young human life was present in Him. A child was born; there is nothing more human than that. Jesus was clearly a real human being, even though we shall need to show later that He was not *only* a human being.

More than human, in fact; the God-human. His birth was human, to be sure, but it has a more than human aspect. We must therefore look again at what happened in Bethlehem. A child was born; that is natural. A Son was given; that is divine (Luke 1:35; cp. Matthew 1:20-23). God comes to humans, as a human. He comes as every human comes, born as a baby, and Mary from Nazareth is chosen for an event that is more than human. The statement in the Apostles' Creed that Christ "was conceived by the Holy Spirit and born of the Virgin Mary" is therefore very fitting, being grounded in the inspired records of God's incarnation. We cannot deal with questions of textual criticism here, but it is important to underline that we have two undoubted, genuine, independent witnesses to this statement in the scriptures, in Matthew 1:16-25 and Luke 1:26-38. And it must also be emphasised that no convincing explanation of the origin of the idea of the Virgin Birth has been given by those who reject the truth of the records and the historicity of the event.

The authority of Matthew and Luke on the subject of the Virgin Birth is unassailable, and they agree that the birth of Jesus was the result of a special work of the Holy Spirit. The silence of the other New Testament writers regarding the Virgin Birth does not cast doubt upon it. No reliable conclusion can be drawn from an argument from silence. Must every New Testament writer authenticate a fact before it can be accepted? Besides, the fact that Mark and Paul did not specifically mention the Virgin Birth does not necessarily mean that they did not know about it. It was clearly not Mark's intention to tell the story of Jesus' birth; he meant only to recount certain events in Christ's ministry from the common apostolic tradition that began with the baptism of John and ended with His being "taken up". He may have omitted the birth narrative deliberately rather than because he did not know of it, and in any case his doing so in no way contradicts Christ's miraculous birth.

The book of Acts does not mention the circumstances of Christ's birth either, yet we know that its author, Luke, knew about it. This confirms his reliability and faithfulness to his sources: he does not put into the mouths of the early Christian preachers a teaching that some of them would not yet have known, even though he himself wants to affirm it. The silence of large parts of the New Testament can also be explained by the circumstances of the event. It is unlikely that Joseph and Mary would have talked about their unusual experiences at Nazareth, especially with other children about the house. It was only as the Church became aware of how the birth had happened that people would have seen how appropriate it was for the incarnation of the Son of God. And even then they would have focused on the central fact that by the work of the Holy Spirit the Saviour of humanity had appeared in human history. The tendency was, as it should have been, to lose sight of the human channel and pay attention to the result (Galatians 4:4; Titus 2:11; 1 John 3:5, 8).

So the doctrine of the Virgin Birth is essential to the Christian faith. It is not a human hypothesis, but a divine disclosure. It was a fact first, and a doctrine afterwards. When the full truth about Christ is understood, this birth that is at one and the same time human and divine is seen to be in line with the whole New Testament revelation. It is not discovered by faith, but disclosed to faith.

It is in this way that we must read Paul's statement in Philippians 2:6-8. He is sure that in the person of Christ deity has actually broken into humanity. The one who was in very nature God did not consider His equality with God as a prize to be grasped, but emptied Himself, taking the very nature of a servant, and being found in appearance as a human He humbled Himself. What is this except an advanced doctrinal statement of the historical fact of the

Incarnation by supernatural conception and birth that Matthew and Luke record?

There are also some passages in other parts of the New Testament that can be read as allusions to Christ's miraculous entry on to the stage of human history, such as John 1:13-14; 6:42; 8:41-42; Galatians 4:4.

There is no basis for the claim that the Christian doctrine of Christ's person and the Christian experience of Christ's work do not depend in any way on His miraculous conception. Both are closely bound up with the truth of the Gospel records of His coming into the world. No one can read the stories of His birth and see the miraculous conception as an isolated marvel. It is the ground on which the whole spiritual and ethical significance of Christ's person rests. So it is relevant to note the results that follow from the declaration of His unique birth in each Gospel. After the angel tells Joseph that he is not to be afraid to take Mary as his wife, because she is pregnant through the Holy Spirit, he then declares the meaning of the event: "you are to give him the name Jesus, because he will save his people from their sins." The one born in this miraculous way is the Saviour (Matthew 1:21). Luke relates the miraculous birth to Jesus' divine Sonship (Luke 1:35). This birth is therefore a guarantee to us that there is a divine purpose in His coming. A purely "natural" Christ does not require a "supernatural" origin. But the supernatural birth of God's Son as the Saviour of humankind fits well with the heart and meaning of Christianity.

Nor is the miraculous birth unrelated to Christian experience. There is a parallel between Christ's physical birth and our spiritual birth. He alone needed no second birth; He alone is acceptable to God having had only one! In His birth the divine Son of God became united to human flesh, and in our spiritual new birth we are made partakers of the divine nature (2 Peter 1:4). His physical birth and our spiritual birth are both effected by the Holy Spirit.

So there is a parallel between Christ's birth in the flesh and our birth in the Spirit, a parallel that extends to the agent and the result of each event. Christ was conceived by the Holy Spirit and emerged as a new creation from God's hand. And if anyone is in Christ, there is also a new creation, a birth from above. With Christ's birth there was a new beginning, the start of a new era; the old age had passed. And in the same way our spiritual birth by the Spirit effects a new beginning: the old life in the flesh gives way to the new life in the Spirit.

The birth of Christ was a miracle. Someone who has experienced the miracle of the new birth will not lightly dismiss the stories of Christ's supernatural conception. No language can better express the wonder and glory of the Gospel accounts. Wherever Christ is born there is a miracle, a miraculous conception. The birth revealed Him as the Son of the Most High. He was, of course, uniquely the Son of God. But by our spiritual new birth we are accepted as sons of God by adoption and grace (Galatians 4:5; Ephesians 1:5; Romans 3:24; 5:2; 11:5-6). The birth of Jesus brought joy to the angels but aroused the envy and hatred of Herod. A struggle for supremacy had begun between the old order and the new.

Chapter 2

The Development of His True Humanity

His Growth to Adulthood

Jesus did not come into the world as a fully equipped Saviour. He had, as the letter to the Hebrews makes clear, to enter more deeply into our human life and identify fully with our human experiences. He had to make Himself known as the real and the true human. It is in this letter that we find the phrase "in the days of his flesh" (5:7; NIV: "During the days of Jesus' life on earth"). Although it hints at His pre-existence, not in the flesh, it is one of the purposes of the writer vigorously to argue for His real and true humanity. He is fully convinced that Jesus was an historical person who lived, grieved and suffered. The Son of God has come, and as a human being He shared in flesh and blood (2:14, 16-17). He is thus the "Brother" who, like His siblings, depends upon God (2:11-13). He grew and learned as a result of His earthly experiences (12:2, 3). His obedience and suffering (2:9-10; 5:8; 10:5-10), His temptations and sympathy (2:18; 4:15) and His humility (5:4-5) are underlined. Although He was a Son, He learned obedience through the things that He suffered (5:7-8).

We can also see what Hebrews says about Jesus in the Gospels' presentation of His human life. Here is a personality developing though a series of actions: fulfilling His responsibilities, resisting the temptations of evil and surmounting moral crises. We see the maturing life of a person growing to adulthood. He was already the Son and the sinless one, and he grew into His vocation rather than His position or His character; but even so he really grew in insight, in His understanding of the work that He had come to do. In other words, he did not grow in moral stature, but in his embracing of His calling and purpose as the incarnate Saviour.

This is how Jesus' silent years in Galilee must be interpreted. Galilee provided Him with a home where he developed; Judaea gave him a cross where he died. He spent around thirty years in comparative obscurity in the carpenter's house in Nazareth, growing in knowledge, life and love. This period has been described as His true and full human development. It involved outward submission to others and inward submission to God, and it resulted in wisdom, grace and favour. These quiet years were for Him more than a time of preparation for His work; they were in a deeper sense the beginning of it. These thirty years of human life were necessary, so that His divinity might not overshadow or overpower His humanity.

We have only the smallest window into what was going on throughout those silent years in the life and experience of Jesus. But we have enough to show Him to us as a human being. Luke's account includes a general statement about His human development and a specific reference to His awareness of His divine Sonship.

Jesus "grew and became strong; he was filled with wisdom, and the grace of God was on him… Jesus grew in wisdom and stature, and in favor with God and man" (Luke 2:40, 52). The record is not crowded with silly fables of arbitrary omnipotence and magical omniscience, such as are characteristic of the apocryphal gospels. The inspired account presents Him to us as increasing in spirit, mind and body, quietly developing during the silent years.

The account of His visit to the temple also presents Him, too, as a growing boy alive to theological questions (Luke 2:41-50). Those who believe Him to be less than He is cite examples of precocious Jewish youths asking troublesome questions of their teachers, but such instances only serve to demonstrate how "natural" Jesus' boyhood was. Yet although the presence of a questioning youth among the teachers was not unheard-of, those who heard Him were amazed at His insight and answers. And the story does not end there: His reply to His mother shows that He recognised His relationship to God as His Father, and that He Himself had to be about His Father's business (Luke 2:49).

So the silent years were important for the humanity of Jesus, and also for our spiritual growth in Him. Spiritual babies must grow, and we do so after the pattern of His development. Those Galilean years were the period of His growth. He experienced life in Galilee, facing and defeating temptations day by day. His heart grew stronger and his vision clearer, and were met by the rebuffs of others and by defeat and sin in those He loved. He learned how to rise to the growing demands of life. And so it should be for us all. Obedience to the purpose of God became His food even then; and for us too it is our obedience that makes us mature, not the mere passing of the years. Those silent years were a time of learning, as He discovered truths about Himself and the world; and those who are born again into His world also discover new truths. Those thirty years were also a period of discipline. Even then He did not do as He wished and was becoming aware that He was being tested. He accepted restrictions willingly. He had to face the jeers and misunderstanding of His brothers. As He grew, the division between them and Himself was becoming clearer and wider; and yet He still loved them. Thus He developed through the years and assumed His appointed task as a real and true human being.

His Human Maturity

"The chief end of man," declares the Westminster Catechism, "is to glorify God and enjoy Him for ever." Only someone who fulfils this high purpose is a true human being. It is precisely here that we see Jesus' mature humanity. He is above all others a human who lived for God, fulfilling humanity's goal of glorifying God.

The fulfilment of this goal required Jesus to meet every righteous demand and to resist every evil temptation. In this respect His baptism and temptations are important. In the baptism He does publicly what He has always done: He fulfils all righteousness. At the temptations He does again what He has always done: He resists all evil. There is, of course, more in these two experiences than we can ever fathom. But we know that His baptism was important and His temptations real. In both He revealed Himself as a human being who made it His chief end to glorify God. And in both experiences He revealed that He is the mature human being, humanity as it is meant to be.

The baptism in the Jordan (Matthew 3:13-17; Mark 1:7-11; Luke 3:21-23; John 1:29-33) is an act of Jesus' maturity. He is about to take up His life's work, and in this way He declares His intention publicly. Here He offers up His life to God, consecrating it fully to Him. Jesus showed His real and true humanity by submitting to John's baptism, thus "fulfilling all righteousness". In His baptism Jesus vividly expressed His identification with humanity. He identifies Himself with the people who had come to Jordan confessing their sins. He will publicly renounce the sin that He has always renounced in deed and attitude. At the Jordan He openly unites Himself with human sin; at Calvary He will openly atone for it. As a human being He takes His place alongside sinful humanity and enters on His task with the seal of God's approval and acknowledgement upon Him. He has been dedicated to His work in the waters of baptism and anointed with the Spirit for the fulfilment of it.

Of course, His more than human nature needs also to be authenticated. The voice from heaven declares, "This is my Son, whom I love; with him I am well pleased" (Matthew 3:17). This rules out any adoptionist view of Christ's deity. The deity of Jesus is not that of a mere human, indwelt or vindicated by God. The heavenly voice confirms His divine Sonship, and His obedience in baptism attests His authentic humanity.

Evidence of human maturity includes the facing and fighting of temptation, learning to deal with the subtleties and strategies of the devil. In the account of the temptations Jesus demonstrates these qualities. No doubt this was not His first encounter with Satan, nor would it be His last. As Luther characteristically remarked, "Jesus had to work hard to keep Satan at bay." Jesus will defeat Satan throughout, and He will eventually destroy him at length. But in the temptations we see Satan's most focused attack. The time and the place (after the dove, the devil; after the waters, the wilderness) are psychologically appropriate, one might even say devilishly fitting. The ecstasy of a great spiritual experience is often followed by a severe experience of the devil's power.

Jesus had, during the silent years, come to maturity in stature, in wisdom and in favour with God and others. The devil then assails this maturity. The stages of the temptations typify the whole range of satanic assault on human beings through body, mind, and spirit (Luke 4:1-13; 1 John 2:16). All the messianic temptations are focused here; the devil is said to have completed every temptation. The devil fails to conquer Jesus in the wilderness and leaves Him for a season, just as calm follows the storm (Luke 4:13). But He returns with the same temptations, because there are no more. What Jesus had resisted in the wilderness He will resist again in daily life and on the cross. The same temptations will be renewed: to become king by supplying bread, to come down from the cross to induce belief. He will endure the same temptations to take the short-cut, to avoid suffering, to gratify the sign-seekers, to accept worldly kingship. Gathered into the one terrible ordeal in the wilderness were all the assaults of the tempter, to satisfy His bodily cravings, to use His own wisdom to initiate the kingdom and to presume on the care of God. Make these stones "bread": the word has an immediate appeal to a hungry person. Esau had sold his birthright for a bowl of stew; Jesus will face the same temptation; but He will not sell His. He answers

Satan's suggestion by declaring that one does not live on bread alone, but by every word that comes from God's mouth (Matthew 4:4; Luke 4:4; cp. Deut. 8:3); He is the true human, and He has made it His chief end to glorify God. The devil showed Him an easy way out of His circumstances, and into the devil's clutches. It was so simple, so natural; just satisfy your bodily desires. Be selfish!

The second temptation (following Luke's account) is to avoid the cross and to assure Himself of victory. A treaty with the devil will guarantee a triumph over the world. Be successful!

The third temptation turned on the suggestion that He might glorify God by some dazzling feat, such as casting Himself from the temple pinnacle, and thereby mesmerise the masses into belief. It was the temptation to do God's work in His own way; to do some great thing on His own account. Be spectacular!

But Jesus was unmoved by each approach. The devil left Him, and angels came to minister to Him. It is always our relationships after temptation that prove whether we have triumphed or not. Jesus was tempted as a human, and as a human He triumphed. There was no play-acting here. This was no sham fight. He felt the stress of struggling and resisting. There was no escape for Him from the temptations which assail humankind. The one who was made like His brothers and sisters in every way (Hebrews 2:17) was tempted in every way as we are. The question is not whether it were possible for Him to sin, or even whether it were possible for Him not to sin. The question is: did He come out of his encounter with the devil in the wilderness fully victorious? The answer to that is clear and unequivocal: He did.

He who had been baptised to fulfil all righteousness now resists all temptations. He had no secret weapon. He did not call on any means to overcome the devil other than those at the disposal of us all. By the Spirit He was led into the wilderness; in the conflict He used the sword of the Spirit, which is the word of God (Ephesians 6:17). That was all He used; and that was enough.

Mature and assured, He went forth to His ordained task to be for us the one Mediator between God and humankind, Christ Jesus, Himself human.

Humanity under the Spirit

The references above to the action of the Spirit in Jesus' birth, baptism and temptations raise the question of the place of the Spirit in His life and ministry. It seems clear that Jesus experienced an indwelling of the Spirit to perfect His human life and an endowment of the Spirit for the fulfilment of His work as Messiah. The effects of the Spirit were, that is to say, related to both His person and His ministry.

John 3:34 says that the Spirit was given without measure. The text does not explicitly say that the Spirit was given *to Him* without measure, but the arguments to this conclusion are overwhelming. All that He needed because of His human nature was imparted to Him fully by the Holy Spirit.

The Spirit's indwelling and enabling went together with the development of Jesus' humanity, and were the cause of this development. Jesus needed the gift of the Holy Spirit to enable His human nature to be His instrument, in increasing measure, in the working out of His purpose. And all that He needed was bountifully supplied. Born of the Spirit, He grew in spirit (Luke 2:40). The Spirit who ensured that His human flesh, derived from Mary, should not become a base of operations for sin, also made certain that He would progress in spiritual and mental development and advance in holiness and knowledge. The Holy Spirit not only endowed the human nature of Christ with all its necessary equipment, but He also caused these to be increasingly – and eventually fully – used. During His days in the flesh, Jesus experienced the constant and penetrating work of the Spirit. It was under the Spirit that Jesus carried out His duties in the carpenter's shop in Nazareth, and there submitted to the rule of His earthly home. He was prepared by the Spirit for the time of His appearance in Galilee to fulfil His messianic office. In and by the Spirit He fulfilled all righteousness and resisted all temptation, and in the power of the Spirit He returned into Galilee (Luke 4:14).

At His baptism Jesus was consecrated for His office by the Spirit's descent in the form of a dove, to provide the necessary inner strengthening and equipping for His task. The outward symbol was not for His sake, but so that others might see and hear the evidence of His commissioning and declare what they had seen and heard. Under the Spirit He has grown to maturity, and now He goes away freshly anointed to do His messianic work. Coming into Galilee in the power of the Spirit, He will remain in that power and He will live a life of obedient service under that power. For the Spirit that descended upon Him at the baptism "remained on Him" (John 1:32).

It is important, therefore, to note our Lord's own declaration in the synagogue of Nazareth, when He applied to Himself the words of Isaiah 61:1: "The Spirit of the Lord is upon me", anointing Him to preach and to fulfil the messianic work listed in this prophetic passage (Luke 4: 17-19). Jesus carried out every function of the messianic office in the power of the Spirit. And since the Holy Spirit is the divine instrument of the mighty acts of God, it is unsurprising that Jesus lived His life and fulfilled His divine mission through the Spirit's power. This point is that Jesus could neither do anything (John 5:19, 30; 8:28) nor say anything (John 3:34; 7:17-18; 8:28) by Himself. He cast out Satan by the Spirit of God (Matthew 12:28), and He declared the words of God through the same Spirit (John 3:34). Thus the Spirit remained with Him throughout His earthly life, controlling His mind, will and actions so that He learned from God, acted for God and taught in God's name in the fullness of the stature of a perfect human. In the end He offered Himself through the eternal Spirit (Hebrews 9:14). Even after His resurrection it was through the Holy Spirit that He gave instructions to His chosen apostles concerning His continuing purpose in the world (Acts 1:2). There is no strangeness, no incongruity, therefore, in Peter's declaration in the house of Cornelius that Jesus of Nazareth was anointed "with the Holy Spirit and with power"; and with that anointing and in that power He lived a life that was pleasing to God, going about doing good (Acts 10:38). This intimate relation and association between Jesus and the Spirit fits well with the biblical statement of the connection between the risen Jesus and the Spirit today. Pentecost was won for us at Calvary; thus "he has received from the Father the promised Holy Spirit and has poured out what you now see and hear" (Acts 2:33). No-one knew better than Jesus how much His people needed the Spirit for their life and work. When, therefore, He went away, He sent the Spirit to equip the saints for the work of ministry (Ephesians 4:1-13).

Chapter 3

The Challenge of His Perfect Humanity

The Sinless Human

The Jesus who fulfilled all righteousness and resisted all temptation, the human Jesus, in every moment and circumstance of His earthly life under the Spirit, is presented in the Scriptures and confessed by the Church as the one perfect human being whom the world has ever seen and known.

We have already noted that in the early days of the Church there were those who believed that the flesh is sinful in itself, and who as a result denied the reality of Christ's physical body. The claim by some writers that Paul's teaching gives support to such a view can safely be discounted. It is true that the apostle closely associates sin and the flesh (e.g. Romans 6:6; 8:3), but he uses the term "flesh" (*sarx*) in a twofold way. In the great majority of cases it has the sense of human nature conditioned by the body. In 35 of the 91 occurrences, however, the apostle gives it an ethical significance, as human nature conditioned by the fall. It is in this context that he relates sin closely to the flesh, as, for example, in his statement that "nothing good dwells within me, that is, in my flesh" (Romans 7:18, NRSV). But nowhere does Paul say that the "flesh" is itself sinful. It is that part of human nature that most readily gives sin its opportunity; it is the part that sin exploits and uses as its base of operations. Identification of sin and the flesh is impossible in light of Paul's teaching that the body can be cleansed and sanctified (1 Corinthians 6:13, 19-20; 2 Corinthians 7:1; cp. Romans 6:13; 12:1). The apostle certainly insists on the reality of Christ's body (Colossians 2:9ff.) and at the same time maintains His sinlessness (2 Corinthians 5:21), thus making clear that flesh is not sinful by its very nature.

In the Bible sin is not conceived as a spiritual disease hiding in the blood of the mother and received into the veins of the child. Sin is essentially moral and spiritual, not material and tangible. The Church has always set itself against any identification of sin with our material substance. Sin is not essential to humanity; it is an intruder. The more sinful someone is, the less human that person is; the less sinful someone is, the more truly human that person is. The sinlessness of Jesus confirms the claim that He is perfectly human.

On the other hand, we have also noted that in the early centuries of the Church there were those who placed the seat of sin in the mind and therefore denied that Christ had a human mind, replacing it with the divine Logos or Reason with its divine power set aside. But to ascribe such a truncated humanity to Christ makes pointless the biblical injunctions to believers to have the mind of Christ (1 Corinthians 2:16; Philippians 2:5).

The life of Jesus was authentically human. It was also distinctively and uniquely human, but only in respect of those characteristics that make the rest of us less than human. He alone lived a sinless human life. The records of that life betray no attempt to make Him seem better than He really was. They do not set out to "prove" His sinlessness. They tell the story without pretence, simply describing how He lived out His life. The Synoptic Gospels do not claim explicitly that Jesus was morally pure, and neither do they set out to prove His innocence or to eulogise Him. They give an account of His life as He lived it, and that is enough.

Yet as we follow the account we see how He withstood the scrutiny of both friends and enemies. His very presence was a rebuke, a cause of shame in others (Matthew 3:14; 27:19; Luke 5:8; 23:47; John 19:6).

The Jesus of the Gospels knew more about sin than anyone; yet He never displayed the least consciousness of it in Himself. He saw, rebuked and forgave sin in others; He grieved over it and suffered for it; He knew what was in everyone, yet He could issue the challenge, "Can any of you prove me guilty of sin?" He had no memory of being defeated by sin, no scars caused by His own sin, no shame from a bad conscience. He lived His whole life with no sense of guilt and no fear of suffering the consequences of His own sin. The question of Mark 10:18 ("'Why do you call me good?'") cannot be taken as a veiled confession of wrongdoing. The adult life of Jesus, as depicted in the Gospels, was entirely free from any trace of sin, so that in His case there was no disordering of human nature or natural sickness of soul, such as we experience from the beginning (Luke 1:35).

As we examine the New Testament we find overwhelming testimony to the fact that sin found no foothold for its evils in Christ. Those who were most intimate with Him and closest to Him were unable to record any blemish. John, who said that if we say we have no sin, we deceive ourselves (1 John 1:8), deliberately excludes Christ, whom He Himself knew (1 John 3:5). Paul is no less confident that His redeeming Lord is a sinless Saviour (2 Corinthians 5:21).

The letter to the Hebrews, more than all the other New Testament writings, uses the sinless perfection of the human Jesus as the basis for a sharp contrast between the old covenant and the new (Hebrews 7:26; 9:14). In the very passage where His equality with us in respect of temptations is asserted, so also is His difference from us in respect of sin (Hebrews 4:15). The apostolic writers certainly regarded Jesus as sinless and holy. He not only kept Himself free from sin in his words and actions; he also pleased God in all the requirements that are laid upon human beings. And these apostolic writers were God's chosen interpreters of His saving purpose in

Christ. They knew that the one who had been appointed to perform such a great task was holy in every aspect of His life. This conviction was not an intrusion into the revelation, but part of it, for they conveyed the message of God's grace; they did not corrupt it.

Only a sinless person could channel and guarantee divine forgiveness. So if Jesus is to achieve salvation for us, then He must be free of the taint of evil. The analogy with the unblemished lamb of the Old Testament relates the sinlessness of Jesus directly to God's redemptive work. A whole series of passages directly influenced by Isaiah 53 unite the Servant of the Lord with the sinless Jesus of the Gospels to show that He, on whom the Lord lays our iniquities, is without any Himself (1 Peter 2:22; cp. Acts 3:13-14; 4:27, 30).

The human Jesus is thus the true, normative human being, the one sinless person. But the fact of Jesus' sinlessness has produced in His followers, throughout the history of the Church, not a claim to perfection, but a sense of imperfection. Sinful humanity is hardly the source or model of this sinless human figure. In every way His life is what human life was meant to be. He loved God with His whole mind and heart and soul and strength, living a life of perfect worship. He fulfilled all the conditions of a blessed life, making real the beatitudes that He taught to His disciples (Matthew 5:3-12; Luke 6:20-23). He took a towel and demonstrated that He had taken the place of lowly service. The description of love in 1 Corinthians 13 can be taken as a vivid portrait of His life of perfect love. The consecrated life outlined in Romans 13 was incarnated in Him. His sinless life is a greater miracle than any of the others He performed.

The Significant Human

The figure of Jesus as it is presented to us in the Gospel story and interpreted to us in the rest of the New Testament is not that of an unearthly, angelic visitor or a demigod in human shape. It is that of a real human being who lived a perfect life in the context of our common human experience. It was as a human that Jesus came, lived and died. It was as a human that He emerged from the darkness of the tomb after three days. After the resurrection He still bore the marks of the nails, and with these His disciples saw Him go up into heaven. At the right hand of God is a real human being, glorified. Here is comfort for the faithful: at the throne of God we are understood; mercy still has a human heart and a human face. Christ as a human stands beside God for us. He knows every twist and turn of our human journey, and He still cares for us. He has lived at our human level and understands our human nature. He has shared so intimately with us that He can sympathise with us fully.

This perfect human is the ideal for our faith. The world has always dreamed of the coming of a perfect human. The vision of a perfect human satisfies the world's ideals. Christianity alone presents what all have sought for. And whatever surprises may be in store for the world, Jesus will never be surpassed. He is the realising of all that is true and right, the perfection of all beauty, the summit of all character. The Gospel alone holds out to the world the reality of the perfect human: perfect in body, so that miracles sprang from His hand; perfect in mind, so that truth flowed from His lips. All humans are measured by this perfect human.

We cannot label Jesus or drag Him down to our level. Other people are noted by one or two outstanding characteristics: one is brave; another is kind. But in Him all of these blend into one glorious harmony. Qualities that in others would contradict one another are woven together in Him. Braver than anyone else, He was also humbler than anyone else; familiar with sorrows, He was also full of joy; fearless in unmasking sin, He was also gracious with sinners.

For humanity, Jesus as the ideal human is both the measure of our failure and the object of our hope. The ideal that he embodies is such that no-one, however much we may strive, can ever attain to it in this age. It always points up the contrast and conflict between what we are and what we ought to be. Jesus the perfect human, the human ideal, thus demonstrates the extent of human falling short and human need. It is in this way that our awareness of the perfect humanity of Jesus becomes the stepping-stone to faith. The personality of Jesus defies comparison and shows how futile it is to treat Him as a mere example. As an example he is beyond human attainment. So to see the perfect human as He is revealed in the Gospel records is to see someone who cannot ultimately be assessed in human categories. He truly stands alone. To be like Him is the Christian's highest hope; to meet Him is the sinner's greatest fear. Jesus has no peer and no replica.

It was because He was really, truly and perfectly human that we must press on. Never before or since has there been anyone like Him. In the light of His eyes is the glory of God, in the fragrance of His personality the sweetness of heaven, in His kingly bearing the majesty of the eternal, in the wounds of His body the divine marks of a love everlasting, in his strong, uplifted arm the saving strength of the Godhead. Such a human being must also be more than a human being. Since He embodies an ideal that contrasts Him with other people, He presents Himself as something more than a leader of people. We desire not someone who can only rouse us to troubled exertion, but someone who can give us peace. A Christ who is nothing more than an unattainable ideal and an embodied law is insufficient to meet our need. Such a person would be little more than a lovely picture, and his Gospel no more than a story of someone who lived well long ago but is no longer with us.

But if we see Jesus as the perfect human, then if we look closely, we will see Him as more than this; we will feel the need of someone who was more than a perfect human long ago, someone who is a perfect human here and now. We need a Christ who is alive, so that he can still help us in our weakness; and so, because of our need, we must look at Jesus again, to see if He is not something more than our example, heartening and yet disheartening.

The Son of Man

In the past the title "Son of Man" was often taken to refer to Christ's human nature, while the title "Son of God" referred to His divine nature. The term "man" made this equation natural, and in some places Jesus' use of the title certainly does signify His human nature. For example, in Mark 2:27-28 Jesus asserts that as Son of Man He is Lord even of the Sabbath. The Sabbath is made for humankind, not humankind for the Sabbath. Here Jesus identifies Himself with human beings and defends their rights as such, while at the same time indicating His supremacy over them. Another possible example is found in Matthew 11:19, where Jesus contrasts Himself with John the Baptist, the austere wilderness preacher, with the words: "The Son of Man came eating and drinking." Is He here signifying His appreciation of all the natural and simple enjoyments of human life? On the strength of such passages some readers still prefer to understand the title "Son of Man" as expressing His deep connection with humanity.

There is no need to demonstrate that Jesus' sense of identity with humankind was a motivating factor for Him. He had the fullest and deepest sympathy for everything that is highest and holiest in human nature and destiny. His compassion reached down to all that is most pitiable and painful in our human lot. He is without doubt the brother of all humans, and the definitive human being. But the instances of the title that clearly refer to His humanity are comparatively few. The very title that includes the word "man" in fact presents Him to us as more than human.

It is well known that the title "Son of Man" was Jesus' most frequent designation for Himself. He seems to have preferred it to all others. He might acknowledge other titles, or at least not repudiate them, but this one was His favourite, and on His own lips it almost eliminated others (apart from "Son of God", which He used less frequently).

The title is found 70 times in the first three Gospels, and it appears as early as Mark 2:10. Although its use becomes more frequent towards the end of the Gospels, it was clearly on the lips of Jesus from the beginning of His ministry. After Peter's great confession it appeared to gain a deeper significance with a wider public. We may set aside the suggestion that the phrase was no more than an equivalent for "I", or that it meant merely "the ideal man".

Yet Jesus never defined the title; nor did He indicate its source. It occurs frequently in the Old Testament (e.g. Psalm 8:4; 80:17), and especially in Ezekiel, where 90 times it refers to the prophet himself. But it is generally believed that Daniel 7:13 is the source of the title: the vision of one like a Son of Man who receives a kingdom. The title also occurs in the Similitudes of Enoch and 2 Esdras (although its use there may not be pre-Christian). In the first of these references the figure of the Son of Man, who is from of old and appears as a celestial being, is definite and personified. It cannot be said for certain that Jesus drew upon this circle of ideas in using the title for Himself. Perhaps He derived it partly from the Old Testament and partly from His own messianic consciousness.

It is significant, however, that the use of the title seems to have caused no surprise either among Jesus' disciples or in the public at large. It was evidently a known title, although it does not seem to have been used by the Jews for the Messiah before Jesus came. The question asked by the crowd in John 12:34 concerns not Jesus' use of the title but His statement that as Messiah He must be "lifted up". The juxtaposition in this passage of the terms "Messiah" and "Son of Man" make clear that by this time the latter had acquired a messianic significance.

In using this title for Himself Jesus was asserting that He was in the world to fulfil a divine mission in connection with the messianic kingdom. He seems to have preferred the title to that of "Messiah", possibly because it did not carry the same associations to His Jewish contemporaries of military and political leadership. But the title acquired a more definite messianic connotation as Jesus became more and more able to unfold to His disciples His messianic calling and purpose. The further He disclosed His Messiahship, the more frequently did He use the title "Son of Man". The first open admission of His messianic vocation is definitely associated with the term (Mark 8:27, 31ff.; Luke 9:18, 22ff.; cp. Matthew 16:13, 21ff.).

The passages in which the title is found show that it combines the ideas of suffering and glory. There are several references in which the thought of suffering is uppermost (see for example Mark 8:31, par. Luke 9:22; Mark 9:9, par. Matthew 17:9; Mark 9:12, par. Matthew 17:12; Mark 9:31, par. Matthew 17:22; Mark 10:33, par. Matthew 20:18/Luke 18:31-32; Mark 14:21, par. Matthew 26:24/Luke 22:22; Mark 14:41; Matthew 12:40, par. Luke 11:30; Matthew 26:2; Luke 22:48). Passages that show the Son of Man in the context of triumph and glory are no less numerous (see, for example, Mark 8:38, par. Luke 9:26; Mark 13:26, par. Matthew 25:31/Luke 21:27; Mark 14:62, par. Matthew 26:64; Luke 22:22; Matthew 13:41; 16:27-28; 24:27, par. Luke 17:24; Matthew 24:37, 39, par. Luke 17:26; Matthew 24:44, par. Luke 12:40; Luke 12:8; 17:22, 30; 18:8; 21:36).

So when the title is understood in terms of its distribution and contexts it conveys Jesus' oneness with humankind as the real, representative and typical human. But alongside this sense of oneness with humanity is also that of Jesus' uniqueness among humanity, in virtue of His appointment to future glory and universal sovereignty. This primary meaning was enriched, especially in the closing stages of Jesus' ministry, with the thought of suffering. Humanity and future apocalyptic triumph thus combine to make the title "Son of Man" supremely interesting and important. Jesus calls Himself "Son of Man" against the background of Daniel 7:13, which refers to a kingdom; and it was as founder of the kingdom of God that He came like a Son of Man. "The Son of Man must suffer" ... "When the Son of Man comes in his glory"; here are united the ideas of suffering and sovereignty. The humiliation is offset by the exaltation. The King comes to the throne by way of the cross. Humility and majesty meet and blend in the character and experience of this Son of Man.

The dozen or so references to the title in John's Gospel reflect a theology that not only presupposes but also amplifies the messianic significance of the title for the person of the incarnate Christ. The element of supernatural pre-existence is primarily emphasised (John 3:13 etc.).

The two connotations of the title correspond to Old Testament descriptions of the Messiah: His lowliness as the Servant of Yahweh and His lordship as God's vice-regent. In the Old Testament these two lines of prophetic anticipation never meet; it is only in Jesus that their apparent conflict is resolved. Thus the term "Son of Man" both revealed and concealed the glory of a Messiah who suffers and the humility of a King who reigns.

The Divine Reality

"Who do people say
the Son of Man is?"

Chapter 4

The Truth as It Is Revealed

It was at Caesarea Philippi that Jesus put His key questions to His disciples (Matthew 16:13ff.; Mark 8:27ff.; Luke 9:18ff.). The place, the time and the people involved were all significant. The town of Caesarea Philippi, nestling at the base of Mount Hermon, was beyond the direct influence of the Jews. With His eyes towards the great beyond of the Gentile world, Jesus asked a question that centred on His own person. Caesarea Philippi was given its name by Philip the tetrarch, who shrewdly associated his name with that of Caesar Augustus. But neither Philip nor Augustus has had such a significant and saving impact on subsequent centuries as the person who stood there that day with his friends. It was He, not they, who turned the course of the centuries. "Who do people say the Son of Man is?" The question is even more meaningful in light of subsequent history.

The timing was also important. The denouement was at hand. Jesus puts the most searching and important question to His disciples (Matthew 16:15). Their attitude towards Him must be openly revealed. They must be made to commit themselves. Jesus first asks them to state what the "people" think of Him. He is not concerned about the opinion of the rulers. He knows only too well that they are blind to His identity. But the people: they have seen His miracles, heard his teaching, rejoiced at his coming; have they gone further? Have they gained a glimmer of understanding of His person and mission? The disciples list the various ideas found among the crowd (Matthew 16:14).

What of the disciples themselves? In asking about the people Jesus used the title "Son of Man". But have the disciples seen anything of His hidden glory? Have they discovered anything of the majesty that shone through the humanity? Inevitably Peter acts as their spokesman. He makes the great confession: "You are the Messiah" (Mark); "the son of the living God", adds Matthew. Some have asserted that Matthew's extra words are a mere expansion, probably inserted to offset the term "Son of Man". But the suggestion is improbable. The words in Matthew's account express the simple yet profound truth about Jesus. The contrast, if one must be sought, is really with what follows: "Blessed are you, Simon son of Jonah, for this was not revealed to you by flesh and blood, but by my Father in heaven." Christ's use of the phrase "my Father" instead of "God" suggests that the divine disclosure made to Peter related to the paternal and filial relationship between God and Jesus. The verb used for "revealed" is reminiscent of Matthew 11:27, which declares the unique knowledge by the Father of the Son and by the Son of the Father, as well as the unique responsibility of the Son to reveal the Father. Peter's declaration is a concrete example of the revelation of the unique Sonship of Jesus. The contrast is, therefore, between Simon son of John, who knew himself to have a human father, and "the Son of the living God"; Jesus refers immediately to God as "my Father", because He had no human one. Peter's declaration of faith was not the result of human insight, not a discovery made by human wisdom. It was given from above (cp. Matthew 11:27; Luke 10:22). John too recalls that this was his experience; he too knew the truth about Christ through revelation. "We have seen his glory," he says, speaking of himself and maybe including others with him, "the glory of the one and only Son, who came from the Father, full of grace and truth" (John 1:14).

The great confession at Caesarea Philippi is evidently very important. Here Jesus openly accepted the acknowledgment of His Messiahship and clearly asserted a unique Father-Son relationship between God and Himself. So Jesus undoubtedly regarded His ultimate place as on the divine side of reality.

This brings us face to face with what has been called "the Great Dilemma". The scrutiny of both friends and enemies has shown Jesus to be utterly true. So can the impression that He gives that He cannot be understood fully in human terms be set aside? He has shown himself to be the perfect human, but are His claims to be more than human false? He has lived in the power of the Spirit of God; so can He blasphemously assert that the essence of His very being involves an unclouded openness of His mind to the Father if this is not so? It cannot be possible.

He was the truth, but He was hounded to death for speaking falsehood. He fulfilled the law, yet they regarded Him as the supreme law-breaker. He was hailed as King but condemned as a traitor. Those who experienced His miracles knew that He was working the works of God, but He is accused of being a sorcerer. He forgave sins but was charged with being an imposter. He demonstrated His deity in many ways, openly and obliquely, but they took Him for a blasphemer. But can He who exemplified every virtue be held to have none? Can the one who shames everyone by His presence disgrace everyone by an unholy disregard for all that is true, good, lovely and pure? This is not the Christ we know. He must be what He claimed Himself to be in word and showed Himself to be in deed. Jesus demonstrated God, illustrated God; He gave God His right name, and Christians have discovered Him in experience to be the right place to meet God. Christians find in Jesus not simply a high doctrine of God or an inspiring faith in God, but the very life and power of God Himself. In Christ they find all that they look for in God. Jesus Christ is all that God can be to us and does all that

God can do for us. He us not merely "godlike"; He is the incarnation of deity. We find God in Christ, not beyond Him. To speak of Him as the perfect human and a human empowered by the Spirit is to speak of Him truly, but not adequately.

So Jesus appears to belong to the divine side of reality. He is of God, from God, for God. But in what precise sense is this to be understood, and on what authority does it rest?

This dual question will find its answer as the facts are investigated, first by looking at Christ's own claims about Himself, and then at the biblical teaching about Him.

The Self-Manifestation of Christ as to His Deity

We cannot, in the space we have, deal in any exhaustive way with all the ideas and questions involved in this subject. All we can do is to indicate the lines along which it may be approached. There are three broad facts that must be taken into account in connection with Christ's testimony to His divinity. His self-consciousness, His self-assertion, and His self-disclosure prove Him to be more than even a sinless and Spirit-controlled human being.

(i) The evidence shows that Christ knew Himself to be uniquely related to God from the beginning. He spoke in the most intimate way of God as His Father and in the most personal way of God as "my Father". The significance of this is increased by Jesus' designation of God as "Holy Father" (John 17:11). He regarded Himself as standing in a special relationship with the God whom He calls the Lord of heaven and earth (Matthew 11:25). He links Himself with God in the intimate "We" of a unique association: "We", both of us, the Father and the Son (John 14:23). This filial consciousness was the constant factor throughout His earthly life. The disciples certainly saw Him at the beginning as a man specially anointed with the Spirit for some divine purpose, which they came to learn was His messianic vocation. But for Jesus Himself the more fundamental fact was that of His divine origin. At the age of twelve He used the words "my Father" with no less intimacy and significance than He did in the Upper Room. And those words used during that early visit to the temple are so natural as to demonstrate His full awareness of His special association with His Father in heaven. This was not the moment of His becoming conscious of His Sonship.

Jesus, as we have seen, is presented in the Gospels as a man empowered by the Spirit. But it is important to emphasise that there is no causal connection between His Spirit-baptism and His Sonship. He did not become a Son as a consequence of His receiving the Spirit. The truth is rather that He was baptised with the Spirit because He was already the Son. The coming of the Spirit relates to His messianic vocation, not to His Sonship. It is by reason of His Sonship that He is qualified by nature to fulfil His office of Messiah. As Messiah He is called to act in close association with God. He is God's representative, without qualification. Such a purpose and position presuppose a deep and profound oneness of nature that only one who is in the highest sense a Son could adequately fulfil. The office of Messiahship calls for one who is truly Son. On the other hand, because of His Sonship His Messiahship must be of an exalted kind. The high office requires a high person; while the high person will fulfil only an office commensurate with His character and dignity. Thus at the baptism His Sonship was attested by the Father, while in the temptations His Sonship was assailed by the devil.

When we take into account how precise Jesus was in His utterances (Matthew 5: 34, 37; 12:36), and how He Himself admitted to the limitations imposed by His incarnate state on what He could do (Matthew 20:23) and know (Matthew 24:36), then we see how utterly certain and constantly conscious He was of His filial relationship with God. Jesus was aware that His Sonship did not belong only to His earthly existence. He regarded Himself as having being the object of divine love before the world was made. He brought His Sonship with Him from heaven (John 6:38, 46, 62; 8:23, 42). He knew His divine origin deep within Himself. For Him it was natural to regard the end of His life on earth, when His work was done, as a return to the glory that was His in a prior existence (John 14:12, 28; 16:10).

(ii) From what Jesus knew Himself to be, we turn now to what He declared Himself to be. Here we see that His self-testimony is consistent with His self-consciousness. The claims made by Jesus, directly and indirectly, are astonishing in their implications. Yet they are not obviously excessive; they somehow ring true.

So much could be said here that we can allow ourselves only the barest statement of the most important facts.

Some of Jesus' direct claims put him unquestionably on God's side. He declared His Sonship to God as His Father, and those who heard understood Him to be asserting His equality with God (John 5:18). On another occasion He explicitly claimed this equality with God (John 10:30). The honour due to God He regarded as due to Himself (John 5:22, 23).

In some important passages Jesus makes astounding claims that begin with the phrase "I Am". This phrase recalls the Old Testament and suggests that Jesus was obliquely identifying Himself with Yahweh, the great "I Am" of Exodus 3:14. The declarations themselves relate broadly to what Jesus can claim to be in Himself: for example, "I am the way, the truth and the life"; "I am the resurrection and the life"; and so on. Life comes from God, and it cannot be maintained and understood apart from God. Jesus asserts that He too has the prerogative to give life: "even so the Son" (John 5:21). All life, both physical and spiritual, exists because of Him (cf. John 1:3; see Colossians 1:16, 17; Hebrews 1:2).

Other "I Am" statements make the claim that Jesus can be and do for humans what God alone can be and do for them. "I am the true bread"; "I am the good Shepherd". This last claim is especially significant, because it indicates that the Jesus of the New Testament is the same to His people as the Yahweh of the Old Testament was to His (cp. Psalm 23:4; Isaiah 40:10-11; Ezekiel 34:11-17; also John 10:1ff).

Throughout the Gospels Jesus calls people to service and sacrifice, even to death, "for His sake". This is a bold demand, but it is reinforced and becomes credible in light of the Old Testament prophets' and psalmists' phrase, "for the Lord's sake", or more usually "for His name's sake". By deliberately substituting the words "for my sake", Jesus was clearly putting Himself in the place of God.

Over and over again we find Jesus making assertions that, although they are extraordinary, do not seem exaggerated, unreal or absurd. They carry the quiet certainty of divine authority. He will build His Church and no opposition will frustrate His purpose (Matthew 16:18). To confess His name is to be blessed by Him and to be accepted by His Father in heaven (Matthew 10:32, 33; Luke 12:8, 9). He identified the word and will of God with His own word and will (Luke 6:46-49; 11:27-28; Matthew 7:21-29; 12:49, 50). He asserted on the authority of His own Name a new commandment (Matthew 5:43ff.; Luke 6:27 ff.). His use of the expression "I tell you the truth" was a deliberate substitution for the prophetic "This is what the Lord says". Thus can He speak in His own name the word of God. The prophets spoke for God; He will speak as God.

Jesus presents Himself throughout the Gospels not first as a prophet but as the subject of all prophecy. No prophet ever dared to make himself not merely *a*, but *the*, subject of not only his own prophecy but also that of others. But this was assumed and asserted in the case of Christ (Matthew 1:22; 26:24; Luke 18:31; 24:25-27). Jesus made soteriological and eschatological claims of the highest order. He had come, He maintained, to give His life as a ransom for many (Matthew 20:28; cp. Mark 10:45). His body broken and His blood shed are for human salvation (Matthew 26:26ff.). He must die, but He will rise again (Matthew 16:21; 17:9, 23; Luke 13:32; John 10:17-18). He declares that all authority has been given to Him (Matthew 28:18) and that He will come again (John 14:3, 18, 23, 28 etc.).

Particular note should be taken of one claim that illustrates a fundamental theological principle, that only by God can God be made known (Matthew 11:27; Luke 10:22). In their ultimate relationship and being, no one knows the Son except the Father, and no one knows the Father except the Son. It is our relation to Jesus that assures our destiny, and in the end it is by Him that we are judged.

(iii) It remains just to add a few words on the third aspect of the present subject: the self-disclosure of Christ, what He showed Himself to be. Here it should be observed that Jesus demonstrated both a knowledge that was unique and a power that was divine.

We have noted how Jesus was truly human and how He grew in wisdom and knowledge. He asked questions in the temple at the age of twelve and continued to do so throughout His earthly life (Matthew 9:5; Luke 18:41; 24:17; John 11:34 etc.). No doubt many of His enquiries were simply a means of beginning a conversation. At the same time He evidently and sincerely sought information on some occasions.

On the other hand, being more than human, He exhibited a knowledge beyond the human. His disciples were convinced, through their experience of Him, that He knew all things (John 2:25; 16:30; 21:17). And this conviction was grounded on His own self-disclosure. He demonstrated that He did indeed know what was in everyone and needed no one to tell Him (John 2:25). He saw the true heart of Nathanael (John 1:47), and of Peter (John 1:42), and of the eager young ruler (Mark 10:21), and of the woman who was a sinner (Luke 7:37ff.), and of His opponents (Matthew 12:25; Mark 2:8). Instances such as these could be multiplied, and others added, to show that the knowledge of Jesus extended to external matters, although always in the service of His moral purpose (John 1:50; 4:39; 6:70; Luke 5:10).

It would seem, therefore, that in the twofold nature of the one Christ of the Gospels there is a twofold knowledge. He knew people as their Lord and as their Brother. Being God He knows people from a distance, as it were. He holds the key to their existence. He knows our thoughts from afar. Being human He knows people at close quarters. He has journeyed along our pathway. Peter acknowledged this penetrating and perfect knowledge when he said to Jesus, "You know [*oidas*: by the fact of who you are] all things, you know [*ginōskeis*: by your experience of me] that I love you" (John 21:17).

"Humanity is a great deep," says Augustine; yet Jesus knows what is in everyone. It is this knowledge that gives reality to His love. "Sir," said Dr Johnson to Boswell, "we form many friendships by mistake, imagining people to be different from what they really are." But Jesus was not so deluded. Jesus' knowledge of humanity gives power to His sympathy. As God He knows our created nature and as a human, since He was made like us in every way, He knows our need. If He had only partial knowledge He could not have perfect sympathy. It is His knowledge that makes His authority final. Whatever Jesus declared is not only the right word; it is also the final word. He speaks with final authority concerning God, life, sin, redemption and judgment, and everything else true that is said on these subjects is but a faint echo of His sayings. And it is His knowledge that makes His commands supreme, His purpose victorious and His appeals urgent.

Christ had not only a unique knowledge but also a divine power. We are not thinking here of His miracles. It is in fact open to question whether these were performed by virtue of His being a perfect human empowered by the Spirit or by virtue of His divine nature. We must, however, observe that His miracles were acted parables. Jesus sought to bring all His miracles into the realm of the spiritual. In this sense they become eloquent sermons, preaching His readiness to come to help everyone in need. Unlike the miracles performed by the prophets of the Old Testament those of Jesus were not an alien and occasional addition to His person and vocation. They were profoundly "natural" to Jesus. It is thus important to observe that He did not need to ask for each of His miracles from God by prayer (cf. 1 Kings 17:20ff.; 2Kings 4:8ff.; Joshua 5:13 – 6:27; Mark 6:41; John 6:11). His miracles were, so to speak, the expression of

His total being. They were so much His own that He could communicate His power to others (Matthew 10:8; Mark 6:7; cp. Acts 3:6; 9:34 etc.). The miracles of Jesus were a service performed out of love and grace; yet for all those who had hearts to understand, their nature was such as to bear witness to Him as someone sent by the Father (John 5:36). The miracles of Jesus are part of the nature of Jesus. They demonstrate the blessings of God to humans and they proclaim the saving deeds of the Gospel. They conform to the person disclosed in the record. In a very definite manner they unveil His glory (John 2:11; 11:4).

Throughout His ministry Jesus revealed Himself in such a way as to make the conclusion inescapable that He can be understood only in terms of deity. He forgives sins (Mark 2:5-12; Luke 7:48). Only one sinned against can forgive, and in the last analysis sin is against God (Psalm 51:4). "Who can forgive sins but God alone?" asked the scribes when Jesus declared the paralysed man forgiven (Mark 2:7); their insight was real but their conclusion mistaken. The awareness of the man that he was forgiven is demonstrated by his getting up and walking. Here was Jesus doing the works of the Christ (Matthew 11:2-4). He was disclosing Himself as the bearer of God's salvation, as the power of God for the deliverance of humans. He was doing what God alone can do for humans.

Jesus also showed Himself to be supreme over the temple (Matthew 12:6), over the Sabbath (Matthew 12:8), and over the kingdom of Satan (Matthew 12:24f.).

We have enough evidence before us to draw the conclusion that Jesus' revelation of Himself in what He knew Himself to be, and in what He declared Himself to be, and in what He showed Himself to be, demonstrate that He is a divine person, who came to fulfil a unique vocation. The teaching He gave, the deeds He performed, the commands He gives, the authority He wields, the knowledge He possesses, the position in which He places Himself, presuppose this fact about Jesus at every point. He is just as we know God should be, and just as we feel God would be, in terms of human life and experience. When, therefore, they asked Him if he was the Christ, the Son of God, the Son of the Blessed (Luke 22:70; Mark 14:61-62), He did not hesitate with the answer. He knew that He was; and He said so.

The Biblical Attestation of Christ as to His Deity
(i) In the Preaching of the Church

As we read the fragments of the primitive preaching and proclamation in the early chapters of Acts, we notice that it is all centred upon the person of Christ. The material that provides us with this summary of early Christian Christology comprises Peter's sermon at Pentecost (2:14-40), his address to the people in the temple (3:12-26), his defence before the council (4:8-12) and his sermon at Caesarea (10:36-43). To this may be added the speech of Stephen before the Sanhedrin (ch. 7), and Philip's conversation with the Ethiopian chancellor (8:30-36).

These passages all reveal that the churches had a doctrine of Christ from the beginning (5:28-32). This shows how far from the mark are those who have maintained that Jesus is dispensable from the Gospel. The truth is the very reverse. The main emphasis in the proclamation of these first preachers of the Christian message is not so much what Jesus taught, but who He is. It was because of who He is that they saw value and meaning and relevance in what He did.

Inevitably Peter started from the historical person, with the person he knew and in whose company he had been. While on earth, Jesus was among people as a man approved by God through signs and miracles (2:22). He was anointed by God with special power (4:27). This approval and this anointing declare Him to be both Lord and Christ (2.36; cp. 10.36). The great declaration, "Jesus Christ is Lord," may well be, as has been suggested, the earliest of Christian creeds.

His unique position is attested by His resurrection from the dead and exaltation to the right hand of the Father. The term

"Father" (2:33) comes naturally from the lips of Peter, who must have had in the back of his mind the disclosures in the upper room when Jesus spoke so intimately of "my Father": "I and the Father are one." It is the Jesus whom Peter had known, and who is now vindicated as Lord and Christ, who communicates the power of the Holy Spirit (2:33), heals (3:16) and forgives (5:31), and is ordained to be the Judge of all (10:42). The ringing message of the primitive preaching is thus that Jesus Christ is Lord of all (10:36).

The one place in this material where the title "Son of God" occurs (8:37) is shown by manuscript evidence not to be part of the original text. But if Jesus is not actually called "Son of God" in our present sources, He is presented in such terms as to put Him beyond explanation in human categories. He is seen as seated at the right hand of God, participating in the divine glory and sharing with God in the government of the world (5:31; 10:36, 42). His lordship is specially mentioned (2:20, 25, 34-36; 4:26; 10:36 etc.). In view of the Septuagint (Greek version of the Old Testament) use of the designation *Kyrios* (Lord) as a name for Yahweh, the application of it to Jesus probably suggested to Jewish minds that He possessed a superhuman character (2:24-25, 36 etc.). His sinlessness is strongly asserted (3:14; 4:27). He is the true object of faith (3:16; 10:43) and the giver of salvation (2:38; 3:19- 26; 4:12; 5:31).

As Christ He is the focus of all prophecy: to Him all the prophets bear witness (3:18; 10:43; cp. 2:25; 8.28ff.). As Christ He must suffer (3:18). It is no surprise therefore to find Him identified with the Suffering Servant of Yahweh (3:18, 26; 4:27, 30) and as the Lamb led to the slaughter of Isaiah 53 (8:32ff.). The whole content of the primitive proclamation can be summarised in Peter's own words: "There is salvation in no one else, for there is no other name under heaven given among mortals by which we must be saved" (4:12).

This material consistently maintains that all the spiritual blessings that humans can possess and God can bestow either here or hereafter are because of this Christ who lived, died, rose again from the dead and reigns as Lord. He stands at God's side confronting people with the offer of God's salvation (2:38; 3:18-20).

Jesus is not presented as the first Christian or as the founder of the Christian religion. As the Lamb led to the slaughter and the Lord at the right hand of God, as the Suffering Servant of Yahweh and the Prince of Life, He is the sum total of all that Christianity means. The early churches did not share Jesus' faith; they had Jesus as the object of their faith, and they believed in God through Him.

The preaching of the Church is, therefore, anchored in Jesus, who is not only the Jesus of history but also the Christ of faith.

(ii) In the Teaching of the Apostles

(a) The Petrine Epistles

The Petrine speeches of Acts and 1 Peter contain the same thought of Jesus being delivered to death by the deliberate counsel and foreknowledge of God (Acts 2:23; 4:28; 10:42; 1 Peter 1:2, 20). The prophecy from Psalm 118:22 of Christ as the stone rejected by the builders is quoted (Acts 4:11; 1 Peter 2:6). In the letter Peter's thought may have moved on from Acts in that the article is dropped from the title "Christ"; it is now a proper name.

Although Peter does not use the term "Son", he has the correlative "Father" (1:2), which indicates a unique relationship. The pre-existence of Christ is more clearly emphasised in the letter. He was foreknown before the foundation of the world (1:20), and this statement cannot be understood in a timeless sense, because the next one says that He was revealed at the last times. He was foreknown because He was there to be known before creation.

He is the channel of spiritual worship (2:5), the chief cornerstone (2:6), the shepherd and overseer of souls (2:25) and the chief shepherd who will appear (5:4). In Him we are called to eternal glory (5:10), and through Him God is glorified (4:11); while the believer is called to sanctify Him in the heart as Lord (3:15).

In 1 Peter the trinitarian formula is clearer (1:2), and the work of salvation is conceived to involve the Father, the Spirit and Jesus Christ; while in many passages it is difficult to say if the term "God" is applied to the Father or to Christ.

In this letter Jesus Christ is proclaimed as the sinless Saviour whose sufferings are a pattern for the believer who is tested (2:21, 22; 4:1, 13; 5:9), and the basis on which humanity is redeemed (1:19; 2:24; 3:18). This last reference unites the person and work of Christ in the divine act of human salvation. "For Christ also suffered once for sins, the righteous for the unrighteous, to bring you to God." He the righteous for us the unrighteous; this is the paradox of the cross. He dealt with sin once and for all; this is the perfection of the cross. He died that He might bring us to God; this is the purpose of the cross (2:23-25).

The key word in Peter's second letter is "knowledge" (1:2, 3, 5, 6, 8, 16, 20 etc.). He stresses three great themes, all of them centring on Christ: the Christian life derives from Christ; Christian truth is found in Christ; and Christian hope looks to Christ. By the act of faith believers have come to share in the common salvation that is in the righteousness of God and our Saviour Jesus Christ. The name "Jesus Christ" is here unusually and solemnly reinforced by the prefix "Lord" or "Saviour" or both. Allusion is made to the testimony given to the Sonship of Christ by God the Father at the transfiguration, when the three disciples were eye-witnesses of His majesty (1:16-18).

(b) The Johannine Letters and Revelation

The three opening verses of John's first letter appear to be an implicit commentary on the prologue with which John opens his Gospel. The term "Word" (*Logos*) may well have given the impression to some readers that Christ is a sort of mystical figure. The Gospel had, of course, clearly insisted upon the human personality of the incarnate Word, but whatever doubt remained about the real humanity of Christ, John here seeks to remove. And he does this by an appeal to personal testimony (1:1). The presence of Christ among humans had been audible, visible and tangible. To deny this is to make Christ a liar (4:2, 3; 5:5). Not only does John insist upon identifying Christ with the human Jesus (2:22), but equally he insists upon relating this Jesus Christ to God (5:5). Indeed, so complete is the identification that in such passages as 5:10 and 5:20 it is impossible to say to which of them the writer is referring.

In two verses (3:5, 8), John relates the appearing of Christ to sin and the devil: He came to take away sin and to destroy the works of the devil. Christ is our propitiation (2:2; 4:10), our means of cleansing (1:7) and our advocate (2:1). In contrast, then, with the Fourth Gospel, which elaborates the theme of Jesus as the Christ, the epistles of John take up the theme of Christ as Jesus. What John states in his first letter he presupposes in the two shorter ones: God meets us in Christ, and Christ is Jesus.

The title "Lamb of God" is a recurring one in the book of Revelation, being found some twenty-nine times. The word used for "Lamb" is not, however, the same as that in John's Gospel (1:29, 36). The term used in Revelation does, however, appear in the Gospel (21:15), although there it is not applied to Christ. In 1 Peter He is likened to a lamb (1:19). Revelation, like the Fourth Gospel and the Epistles of John, has the idea of Christ as the Word. He is the Word of God in Revelation (19:13). In the first letter of John He is the Word of Life (1:1). In the Gospel He is the Word absolutely (1:1). The Epistles present Christ as the Life, and to have Him is to have eternal life (1 John 5:11, 12; cp. 1:2).

Revelation, however, is concerned not so much with Christ's Sonship in the past as with His redemption in the present and His kingship in the future. The dominating concepts are that of Redeemer and King. He is the royal Saviour.

It was during His earthly life that He effected our redemption, so the writer refers frequently to His life on earth as the sphere in which the redeeming act was performed and within which His kingly authority operates. So he emphasises the humanity of the Christ, whom he sees in his vision moving in the heavenly sphere, with redemptive grace and in regal glory. He is from the tribe of Judah and the family of David (5:5; 22:16). His death in Jerusalem is specifically mentioned (11:8). Yet the person to whom such mystical terms as Lamb, Lion and the Word are applied nonetheless shares our own nature (1:13). So this book, which exalts Jesus to the throne, does not detach Him from the world. Throughout the whole revelation of the exalted Christ, the historic Jesus breaks through, thereby undermining all theologies that fail to acknowledge the unique significance of His appearance in history.

John, however, also sees Christ above and beyond history and as the moving power of all things. Jesus therefore is set before us in the dual role of Redeemer within history and the Lord of all history. An examination of the passages where the phrase "Lamb of God" occurs will reveal that it unites the two ideas of redemption (5:9, 12; 7:9-10 12:11; 21:27) and kingship or sovereignty (5:6-14; 6:16; 7:9; 22:1, 3). The concepts of vicarious suffering and victorious love are here made one in the person of the redeeming and reigning Christ. At the very heart of God's sovereignty is sacrificial and suffering love.

Through the blood of Jesus salvation is made available to the believer, and it brings with it liberty (1:5), redemption (7:9, 10, 14; 22:14) and victory (12:11). The Lamb has a place in the midst of the throne. His sovereignty relates to the churches (1:1-18). Here Christ is presented as the Alpha and the Omega, the A and the Z, and the whole rich description of Him serves to accentuate His lordship. This most striking imagery is set before us to reveal His dignity and authority. Both the vision (1:12-15a) and the voice (15b-18) serve to reveal His sovereignty. He has the clothes of royalty, the head of glory, the eyes of brilliance, the feet of victory, the voice of majesty and the hand of authority.

His sovereignty, too, relates to the world. The earth-shaking consequences that result from His opening the seals of the scroll are due to the "wrath of the Lamb" (6:16), and His authority extends to the nations (12:5). His sovereignty relates no less to the final victory of God. He is the supreme agent of God's judgments. It is He who comes with great power and glory to judge the world and save His people (17:14-16; 22:20). So the morning star shall arise and the Lamb shall be the light of the holy city. He is the faithful witness, the firstborn from the dead and the ruler of the kings of the earth (1:5). He is King of kings and Lord of lords (17:14; 19:16).

This presentation of Christ identifies Him clearly with the Godhead and necessarily implies His essential deity. He is the object of divine honours. To Him both worship and praise are given in the same way as to God (5:11, 12; 7:10; 22:8, 9). He is served by saints, just like God Himself (20:6). He sits with God on His throne, having the keys of Hades and death. He is the redeemer of humanity, and what a whole God created cannot be redeemed by one who is only half a god. By applying to Him the words of Isaiah 44:6, which in its Old Testament context describes the absolute eternity of Yahweh as the first and the last, John gives to Jesus a position of equality with God. He belongs to the divine realm of existence and as such can call God His Father in a special sense (1:6; 2:27; 3:21; 14:1). The sevenfold perfection of God is ascribed to Him (3:1; 5:6; cf. 1:4; 4:5). He possesses the secret of Yahweh and writes His mysterious Name upon the foreheads of His saints (2:17; 3:12; 14:1). In the final victory of God the kingdoms of this world are His in union with God, the God of heaven, the Almighty (11:15ff.; cp. Matthew 4:8-10).

(c) The letter to the Hebrews

The author of Hebrews ascribes a wide range of terms to Jesus in His work: pioneer, apostle, mediator, high priest, forerunner, guarantor, shepherd. But there is one term in which he seeks to open to us the inmost personality of Jesus and to reveal what He is in Himself. He is the Son of God, or more simply and absolutely, "the Son". The other titles are descriptive of His office; "the Son" is expressive of His essence. While these other terms reveal what He does, His relation to humans, this has reference to what He is, His relation to God.

The letter to the Hebrews clearly expresses what must ever remain essential for Christian faith, the twofold significance of Christ. He is our brother who inspires our love and confidence because He has made Himself one with us in our common life. He is also set apart from humans and has the power to communicate new life and bring us near to God because He is separate from sinners and made higher than the heavens. But there is no speculative Christology in the letter; no formal attempt is made to reconcile these two facts. Jesus is presented as both Son of God and "this man". He is made less than the angels, yet He is more than they.

The Sonship of Christ is fundamental to this word of exhortation. God has spoken to us in one who is Son (*en huiō*); in one, that is, who has the nature of Son. The absence of an article in the Greek fixes attention upon His nature rather than upon His personality.

The Son is the appointed Heir to all things (1:2). He reflects God's bright glory, is stamped with God's character and sustains the universe with God's own power (1:3). The word translated "exact representation" is *charaktēr*, from which we derive our English word "character"; and the word for "person" is *hypostaseōs*, which conveys the idea of essence. Thus the Son of God is the very character of God's essential being: He has the stamp of God's character. Jesus is God thrown on the screen of human life. "In Him all His Father shone, substantially expressed" (Milton).

As Son He has pre-eminence in the universe. He is the agent of creation and the channel of providence (1:3, 10). To Him who can save, to create is but a small matter.

As Son He is superior to the angelic host. To no angel did God ever give the title "Son". Christ could be made a little lower than the angels, because in eternity He was greatly above them.

The writer of the Hebrews is one with Paul in presenting Jesus as holding all things together, as the chain band of all existence, to use a phrase from Philo. To this writer, as to the apostle to the

Gentiles, creation is centred in Christ (Hebrews 1:2; Colossians 1:15ff.). Thus Moses was just a servant in the house, but Jesus is Son over the house. Three times in the letter the term "heir" appears, and in each place the reference is to the Son's final glory as redeemer. The ascension and exaltation of the Son is emphasised throughout the epistle. The idea is usually pictured as the return of a priest from his sacrifice. In solemn procession He passes from the scene of sacrifice, conflict and victory up through the heavens, and in behind the veil, to the innermost sanctuary, and to the seat of power and authority at the right hand of the majesty on high. He enters heaven in the power of that blood, which is His indestructible life (7:16), and there He appears in the presence of God on our behalf, always living to make intercession for us. By His ascension, therefore, He is definitely marked out and installed as Son of God with power (cf. Romans 1:4). As Son of God He will come to judge and to reign (9:27ff.). To the writer, Christ is given a place beside God. He is greater than the sinless angels. It was with Him that God conferred at the creation of the world. The Christology of this epistle is the same "higher Christology" that is found in Paul and John. 1:8 speaks of Him as God, and 1:10 as Lord. Thus the writer must have held a view of Christ's person that made it natural for him to apply to Him the titles "God" and "Lord", titles that he knew well were designations for the supreme Deity.

(iii) Pauline Christology

So much can be said about Pauline Christology that we can do no more here than outline the subject. Two considerations, however, must be kept in mind regarding Paul's understanding of the person of Christ. We are presupposing, first, that what the apostle has to say respecting Him is in essential harmony with the primitive Gospel. Paul did not introduce a strange Christ to the theological world. He was not the originator of another gospel, which was really no gospel at all (Galatians 1:6f.). We reject the view that it was due to Paul that we have, among his other theological accretions, the

Son-of-God Christology. Some believe that he was the first to give to the title a Christological connotation, and that he thereby "Paulinised" the primitive Gospel. The truth is rather that all Paul's central conceptions, including grace, justification and salvation through the blood of Christ, as well as his so-called "higher Christology", came to him straight from the heart of Jesus' message.

The other point to be made is that Paul's Christology was, of course, coloured by the fact that his first encounter with Jesus was with Him as glorified Lord. It is here we find the dynamic centre of His understanding of Christ. Paul first found Christ on his knees, and this intense experience is reflected in all his Christological statements. For the original disciples it was astonishing that Jesus, whom they knew and whose companions they were, and who had been put to death as a common criminal, should now be exalted to the throne of God. To Paul the reverse was astonishing. He had been apprehended by the living Lord on the Damascus road. The person who had so overwhelmed him by the sheer grace of God was declared to him to be the exalted Jesus (Acts 9:5). He now had a place within the realm of Deity. How could this person become flesh and die? This is humility at its ultimate and its most Godlike (Philippians 2:1ff.). For Paul the glory of Christ lay in the humiliation that brought Him within the human sphere to accomplish His divine work of salvation. For the other disciples the glory of Christ lay in His exaltation from the human sphere after He had died a death that was revealed to be on account of human sin (cf. Acts. 2:22, 33).

For Paul the Damascus road encounter was not the confirmation of a theory but the experience of a theophany. The notion that all the elements of Paul's Christology existed as floating ideas in Jewish messianism and oriental myths does not fit the facts. Paul did not gather together all these apocalyptic speculations and on the Damascus road come to a reasoned conclusion by merely adding the name Christ to them. Such a reading of Paul's conversion is as fantastic as it is eccentric, especially in the light of his later service for the Gospel. The truth is that here Paul found redemption through the very Jesus against whom he was fighting. He was in no mood to attach that name to any religious ideas; rather the now exalted Jesus had put His name on Paul (1 Corinthians 6:11; 2 Corinthians 4:5-6; Galatians 1:10, 15, 16, etc.; cp. Romans 6:1-23; 1 Corinthians 7:23; Ephesians 6:6 etc.). He was a "debtor" who owed all he now possessed to Christ and who could acknowledge his infinite debt only by the full dedication of himself to the one who loved him and gave Himself for him. From that moment on the road outside Damascus Paul was Christ's servant, Christ's slave (*doulos*). Paul was the "prisoner of Christ" for ever after, being led through the world in the triumphal procession of the victorious Lord (2 Corinthians 2:14). He was now "in Christ", living by faith in the Son of God who had been accursed for him that he might be declared righteous before God through a righteousness not his own.

Yet Paul's Gospel, "my gospel" as he calls it (Romans 2:16; 2 Corinthians 4:3; cp. 1 Thessalonians 1:5; 2 Thessalonians 2:14; Galatians 2:2), was not something learned at second hand. It came to him directly by the revelation of Jesus Christ (Galatians 1:16). Flesh and blood had not made it known to him; it had come from above (cf. Matthew 16:17). He can consequently declare what he knew personally and dynamically in his own experience: no-one can say that Jesus is Lord except by the Holy Spirit (1 Corinthians 12:3). This was Paul's Gospel, Christ's Gospel, the true Gospel of God (cp. Romans 1:1-4, 16; 15:15-16, 19 etc.).

The transforming experience on the Damascus road brings into focus what was to be the heart of Paul's proclamation through the years. His conscience awakened by the appearance of Christ, Paul's first reaction was the question: 'Who are you, Lord?' The answer came: "I am Jesus, whom you are persecuting."

Who are you, Lord? I am Jesus. This was the startling and staggering revelation. It was on this fact that Paul was to lay emphasis. Jesus, He is Son of God (Acts. 9:20) and Messiah (Acts 9:22). The centre of his Gospel is, as he tells the Corinthians, the proclamation of "Jesus Christ as Lord" (2 Corinthians 4:5).

Although Paul could assert that his Gospel was no borrowed creed, that what he discovered about Christ came not as tradition from those who as apostles were "in Christ" before him, all that he has to say about Christ is at one with the primitive faith. Paul was in no sense the "second founder of Christianity". He was not the second after Christ but one of those "in Christ". It is after all the same Spirit of God who is over all God's gracious purposes for humankind. Paul's emphasis upon the lordship of Christ is in harmony with all that his predecessors in the faith knew of Him. From the beginning Christ was seen as occupying the throne of the universe. He is the cosmic Redeemer and Lord whose universal sway is attested by the fact that God raised Him from the dead, to inaugurate an eternal kingdom. In Paul, as in the earliest sources of the New Testament, Christ's resurrection and exaltation are united with His lordship. It is those who confess that Jesus is Lord and believe in their hearts that God raised Him from the dead, who are saved (Romans 10:9; cp. Romans 8:34; Ephesians 1:19-20; Colossians 3:1).

Paul's theology was therefore essentially the theology of a person in Christ, a person redeemed by the action of the glorified Lord. From the risen Son of God came all the redemption and the moral power needed to transform people into the image of Christ, the perfect Man.

This lordship of the exalted Christ is all-embracing. Over Jew and Greek, rich and poor, He is the same Lord of all and blesses those who call upon Him. To this lordship all will be subject.

The lordship of Christ is also over the Church. The Church is His (cf. Matthew 16:18; Romans 16:16 etc.), as it is God's (1 Corinthians 1:2; 11:22; 15:9 etc.). Here is a relationship that does not detract from God but which rather exalts Christ to the status of deity. It is from this conviction of the absolute Lordship of Christ within His Church that all the ethical demands of the New Testament are derived. Believers are related to Christ as slaves to Master, and their highest ideal is to obey Christ. The inner power controlling all their motives is the overmastering love of Christ who loved them even when they were still sinners (2 Corinthians 5:14-15; Romans 5:8). Bought with a price, they must glorify the Lord who bought them. Christ is therefore "head over everything for the church, which is his body, the fullness of him who fills everything in every way" (Ephesians 1:22).

His lordship extends to the universe and beyond (Ephesians 1:21). He is, to paraphrase Colossians 1:15ff., the perfect image and visible representation of the unseen God. He is the firstborn, the heir of all that the Father has, begotten before the ages; the Lord of the universe by virtue of His begetting and His creative work. For in Him and through Him the whole world was created, things in heaven and things on earth, things visible to the eye, and things knowable by inward perception. His supremacy is absolute and universal. All powers in heaven and earth are subject to Him. This subjection extends even to the most exalted and most potent of angelic beings, whether they are called thrones, powers, rulers, authorities or by any other title. He is first and last. The universe has been created through Him, and He is its final goal. He is pre-existent and self-existent before all creation. And everything is sustained and held together in Him.

However, as exalted Lord He is not far away and indifferent. He is always present within His Church, indwelling the hearts of His redeemed people. He is their never-failing guide, comforter and leader. He is closer than breath, nearer than hands and feet. Prayer is to be made to Him in full confidence that He has the authority and resources to answer (John 14:13, 14). Paul asked the Lord three times to take away his thorn, and it is clear that the "Lord" whom he asked is the Christ he had come to know (2 Corinthians 12:2-10; cp. verse 9). Calling upon the name of the Lord Jesus Christ was virtually a synonym for being a Christian, while doing anything for His sake was the definition of serving God (Acts 9:16; Romans 15:30 [KJV]; 2 Corinthians 12:10; 3 John 7). By Paul's use of the term "Lord" (*kyrios*), the uniqueness of Christ as one who stands in the place of the Yahweh of the Old Testament is revealed (Romans 10:13; cp. Joel 2:32). For Paul, indeed, the title "Lord" has an exalted significance. In fact, it has ceased to be a title and has become the sacred expression of a personal devotion into which he invested the gratitude, love and loyalty born of his redemption by Christ.

In two passages, Romans 5:12-21 and 1 Corinthians 15:44-49, Paul refers to Christ as the second Adam. The title suggests that He is the founder of a new humanity. In Him, as its representative, a new, redeemed humanity is created. The first Adam began a natural history; by him came death; he is a creature and perishable. The second Adam stands at the head of a new humanity; through Him is resurrection. He is from heaven. The contrast between the first Adam, as a living soul, and the last Adam, as a life-giving Spirit, brings out the fact that as such Christ does not belong only to the natural order. He is above nature, because in Him is life. He has life in Himself, and He is capable of communicating it to those who are united to Him by faith. The new principle of life that is His to give is the outflowing of that Spirit of holiness which is the inmost reality of His being.

This reference to the last Adam as a life-giving Spirit raises the question of the relation between the exalted Christ and the Spirit. This, however, is a subject we cannot deal with here at any length, except to say that while Paul does link the Spirit closely with the person of Christ, as the redeeming agent of God in Christ within the human heart, the relation is not one of absolute identity. As the Trinitarian passages make clear (Matthew 28:19; 2 Corinthians 13:14; 1 Peter 1:2; Jude 20, 21), the relation is one of living unity (1 Corinthians 6:11; 2 Corinthians 4:4-6, 14; Romans 8:11; 1 Corinthians 12:3 and 2 Corinthians 3:17 etc.).

Paul never uses the term "Son of God" except with a profound sense of reverence and devotion. He did not believe that Christ's Sonship was acquired or attained. Such passages as Romans 8:32 and Colossians 1:13 cannot be taken to mean that He is Son because He is loved; they mean quite the reverse. He is loved because He is Son.

It is as Son that He came into the world. The suggestion that Paul initiated the Son of God Christology cannot be supported by the one passage that is claimed to support it, namely Romans 1:4. Certainly Paul does here associate the Sonship of Christ with the resurrection. Christ is described as coming from David's line according to the flesh and declared to be the Son of God in power according to the Spirit of holiness by the resurrection from the dead. Does this mean that the Pauline Christ is designated Son of God only after the resurrection? Of course it does not. No such adoptionist Christology can be deduced from this verse; and in any case such an understanding of Christ would be contrary to the whole thrust of the apostle's teaching. The word in the original (*horizio*) signifies that although Christ was Son of God before the resurrection, yet He was openly appointed or declared to humans to be so by this transcendent and crowning event.

For all his emphasis, however, upon Christ as exalted Lord, as cosmic agent, and as Son of God, Paul was not altogether indifferent to the historic reality of the human Jesus. True, he never makes mention of His miracles, His prayer, His faith, His conduct among others. At the same time the view that Paul was so preoccupied with the exalted Christ that he virtually turned Christianity from a faith rooted in history into a mere Christ-mysticism has little foundation in fact. Nor is it true that the letter to the Hebrews was written as a corrective to Paul, as an attempt to re-assert the Jesus of history.

2 Corinthians 5:16 has been quoted to support the assumption that Paul did not bother himself with the figure of Jesus described in the Synoptic Gospels. But the meaning here is not that Paul had no concern for the historical facts of Christ's life, but the important truth that spiritual things must be spiritually interpreted. To know Christ in a fleshly way is not to have a real spiritual understanding of Him. Whether Paul did actually know Christ during the period of His humanity is uncertain, although it does seem likely. It would appear that he is suggesting in this passage that he did formerly

know Him during the days of His flesh in an outward manner, but that now, in contrast, he knows Him in a living fellowship.

In the record of Paul's sermons in Acts there is evidence of his knowledge of the historical facts of the life of Jesus. He was probably well aware from his pre-Christian days of the kind of apologetic for Christ of which Stephen's speech was an example. After his conversion Paul was baptised, and he was certainly not without some knowledge of the Christ whose name he had taken upon himself. He must have become acquainted with some of the facts about Jesus during the three years he spent in Arabia. According to Galatians 1:18, he went up to Jerusalem on a special fifteen-day mission and there he talked with Peter. He went up to interview Peter, literally to 'history' (*historēsai*) him (though that is not good English!). Paul worked for long periods in company with Barnabas, John Mark, Silas and Luke, all of whom were certainly in possession of the facts about the life and teaching of his Lord. It is incredible to suggest that he would not have learned from them something of these matters, or that he was not interested in what the Lord in whom he gloried had said and done. For Paul a saying of Jesus is the highest authority he can quote. Only when he has no commandment as such from the Lord does he issue his own commandment, though he believes himself to be inspired by the Spirit (1 Corinthians 7:10, 12, 25, 40; 9:14).

A study of the letters of Paul reveals his knowledge of the historical Jesus. Much of it is presupposed, for he was writing "from faith to faith" and to be understood by faith. His epistles are not missionary propaganda; they are for the churches that were in possession of the historical facts. There are, however, impressive passages in which he refers to Christ's entry into human history. He was "born of a woman, born under the law" (Galatians 4:4). He set an example of courage under persecution (Romans 15:1-4). He instituted the Last Supper and was killed on the cross. Paul has much to say about His character as outlined in the story of His life. The glory of the believer is to be conformed into the image of Christ; to express, for example, "the meekness and gentleness of Christ" (2 Corinthians 10:1). 1 Corinthians 13 is nothing if not a portrait of the Saviour. Paul not only quotes the authority of Christ but records His unwritten saying: "remembering the words the Lord Jesus himself said: 'It is more blessed to give than to receive'" (Acts. 20:35). Various statements of the Lord find more than an echo in Paul's letters.

For Paul, then, it is a real Jesus who is Lord. And He is Lord for Paul in the very fullest sense. As we have seen, Paul applies to Him without hesitation the term Lord (*kyrios*), which the Septuagint uses to translate the Hebrew "Yahweh" (1 Corinthians 1:31; 2 Corinthians 3:16; 10:17; Ephesians 4:5; 2 Thessalonians 1:9). Furthermore, the Old Testament "day of the Lord" or "day of Jehovah" became for Paul, without any sense that he is doing violence to the truth, "the day of Christ" (Amos 5:18; Joel 2:1; 1 Thessalonians 5:2; cp. 1 Corinthians 5:5; Philippians 1:6; 2 Thessalonians 1:9-10). There is, therefore, no doubt in Paul's mind as to the true status of Christ. He is essentially divine, fully within the sphere of deity. He is the source, equally with God, of all spiritual blessings for the people of God (Romans 1:5, 7; 1 Corinthians 1:2-3; 2 Corinthians 1:2; Galatians 1:3). He does for us what God does and is for us what God is (2 Thessalonians 3:5; 1 Corinthians 1:4-9; Romans1:1-6; Galatians 1:15-16; 2 Corinthians 5:18; 10:8; 13:10; Philippians 3:12-14; 2 Corinthians 12:8-9; Philippians 2:5-11).

He is consequently for Paul the 'image' (*eikōn*) of the invisible God (Colossians 1:15). He is the One in whom God is seen absolutely. For in Him the very fullness of God took up its permanent dwelling in bodily form (Colossians 2:9). He originally possessed Godhead to the full; yet He did not maintain this exclusive state as a prize to be used for His own advantage, but took to Himself human nature and in that state lived a life of obedience even to death on the cross (Philippians 2:7, 8). Does Paul then hesitate to apply to Him the name "God" in the very fullest sense? He has made Him so Godlike that He cannot be less than God. There are, as we have noted, passages in which God and Christ are conjoined very closely. In 2 Thessalonians 1:12, the statement "the grace of our God and Lord Jesus Christ" (author's translation) seems definitely to identify them and thus to assert Christ's absolute Deity. Titus 2:13 (cp. verse 10), which we assume is by Paul, certainly identifies Jesus Christ as our great God and Saviour. Paul's doxology in Romans 9:5 is therefore true to his Christology. It is a much debated question whether the words "God over all, forever praised" are to be taken as a further description of Christ or as a separate doxology referring to God. The structure of the sentence favours the first. It is on dogmatic grounds only that some have refused to allow that Paul is here making an unequivocal assertion of Christ's essential deity. The suggestion that such a declaration must be regarded as "too advanced" for him begs the question. It is our view that God has revealed Himself fully within the closed canon of Scripture and that, therefore, the Christ designated "true God of true God" and of "the same substance with the Father" of the later creeds, is the Christ of the New Testament. So it cannot be reckoned as beyond the faith and proclamation of Paul to make this full and definitive confession of Christ. The words of Romans 9:5 may, then, be taken to read "Christ ... over all God blessed forever", and thus as an explicit assertion of Christ's deity. Such an assertion is only the natural and legitimate climax of Paul's Christology; we have seen the outline of it in what has gone before.

Throughout Paul confesses both God the Father (Romans 8:15) and the Lord Jesus (10:9). The two are not confused; yet they are intimately related. We are thus led on naturally to the great Trinitarian passages of the Pauline letters, in which the work of the Father, Son and Spirit is unfolded in relation to human redemption. God is known as Father, through the Son, by the Spirit (Ephesians 1:3-14; 2:18, 22). But the Trinitarian benediction of 2 Corinthians 13:14 also confirms the unity of the Christian experience of God. It is God who is known as the divine Father, through the divine Son and in the divine Spirit. This is both the authentic voice of revelation and the living reality of experience. When, therefore, we confess Christ's deity, we simply give Him His right name. All New Testament Christology is the unfolding of the proclamation made at His birth: "Mary was the mother of Jesus who is called the Messiah" (Matthew 1:16). He is the anointed one. He is to be given the name Jesus, for He will save His people from their sins (Matthew 1:21). He is the atoning one. And they shall call Him Emmanuel, which being interpreted is "God with us" (Matthew 1:23). He is the abiding one.

Chapter 5

The Titles that Reveal Jesus

The Pre-Existent One

Although the actual title of pre-existent one is not applied to Jesus in the New Testament, all the data for His pre-existence is there. The application of the category of pre-existence to Him was not a mere deduction, made by faith, on the part of the first disciples. We do not believe that the biblical statements regarding Christ were the result of merely human musings. The truth is rather that the apostles were guided by the Spirit of God in making their profound declarations about the Saviour whom they had come to know. This means, however, that in making their statements regarding the pre-existence of Christ the divinely instructed apostles were not going beyond what was already implicit in the Christian faith as it was already proclaimed and experienced.

One aspect of the kingship of the messianic figure of the Old Testament was his close association or even identity with the personal revelation of Yahweh (Isaiah 9:6). In the prophetic utterance of Micah (5:2), the Messiah who comes as ruler from Bethlehem is, at the same time, one "whose origins are from of old, from ancient times".

In what may be called the more popular teaching of Christ as recorded in the Synoptic Gospels, His continued existence to the end of time is clearly stated. But there are also passages in which His pre-existence is either specifically indicated or definitely implied. The titles "Son of Man", as we have seen, and "Son of God", as we shall see, certainly carry the idea that His existence did not begin at Bethlehem. He is the one who was to come (Matthew 11:3), the sent one (Mark 12:6; cp. Luke 7:19; Matthew 21:9; 23:39; John 6:14; 11:27). The question Christ asked the Pharisees concerning the Messiah's relationship to David suggests that in the back of his mind was the consciousness of His pre-existence before His birth from the seed of David (Matthew 22:41-45; Mark 12:35-37; Luke 20:41-44).

By His (apparently) complete silence regarding His human birth and by His seeming refusal to admit enduring ties with His earthly family Jesus may well have intended to force the question on enquiring minds: where then does He come from? (Mark 3:31ff.; Luke 2:48ff.; cp. Mark 6:3; John 8:38, 41). The famous declaration of Matthew 11:27 can hardly have meaning if the existence of Christ, as Son of God, began within the framework of human history. The knowledge that Jesus claimed is of such a kind that it could not have been acquired by a created being within the limits of a life as brief as that of Jesus. A knowledge so intimate of God's inner nature and hidden purpose, which Jesus regarded Himself as possessing, must run beyond the bounds of history and the limits of time to be explained adequately. His history as Son of God was preceded and followed by eternity. Jesus is not simply enthroned within the world's history; He is and He always was the Son of God's love, the everlasting Son of the Father, enthroned at God's right hand, as the key to all history and its judge.

It is sometimes claimed that references to His pre-existence in the Synoptics are scarce and oblique for the reason that the idea had no secure place in Christ's own consciousness. Such "concordance criticism" is not so serious as is seemingly supposed. Is it not rather more legitimate to suggest that the references are few just because the awareness of Jesus' pre-existent glory held such a large place in His thought? Deep things are not usually paraded; the captain is not voluble in the rapids, nor does he talk about seamanship in the storm. It was not Jesus' usual habit to satisfy idle curiosity. He would leave the truth about Himself to be given from above, to be discovered and appreciated through faith in and fellowship with Him. It was, therefore, His custom to charge those He healed and cleansed to keep silence and not to make Him known.

When, however, we turn to John's Gospel, where the audience is not so much the general public as His disciples, the idea of pre-existence is expressly stated. Jesus Himself declares that such a unique relationship exists, a true substantial identity between Himself and the Father, which did not begin with His becoming flesh (3:13; 6:33-42). He co-existed with the Father prior to the days of Abraham (8:58), and before the world was made (17:5, 24). He descended from above (3:17, 19, 31-34) because He was 'from above' (8:23). His pre-existence is maintained throughout the Gospel. The prologue clearly specifies it. He was there as the personal Word when the world was spoken into being and before His becoming flesh (1:1-18). Deity is ascribed to Him throughout, and in such a context the ascription of pre-existence to Him seems natural and necessary. No one has ever seen God, but the only-begotten Son, who is close to the Father's heart, has made Him known (1:18). The faith of the writer in Christ's eternal existence is shared by John the Baptist (1:30). The equality of the Son's nature with that of the Father is stated so clearly that the whole Gospel depicts Him as in communion with the Father before the ages. There is no thought of His Sonship beginning within time; there is no adoptionist or achievement Christology here.

Every one of Paul's letters takes Christ's pre-existence for granted. In some passages, however, it is said to have a soteriological or ethical power and purpose (2 Corinthians 8:9; Philippians 2:5ff.). There are passages where Paul has what has been called a Logos Christology without using the term. In Colossians 1:15-20, for example, Christ is related to the created universe. He is said to be not only prior, but eternally prior, to all creation. He exists eternally, before all time (Colossians 1:17). The passage teaches the supreme royalty of Jesus Christ. He, upon whom all creation depends, is outside the created order. In His pre-incarnate state He is prior to all creatures, and the agent of their coming into existence. Thus He possesses a supremacy, eternal, absolute and universal (Colossians 1:15, 16; cp. Ephesians 1:7-14).

Philippians 2:5-7 is the fullest and most explicit of Paul's statements on this theme. There are perhaps few statements in Scripture that have occasioned more comments than this. Leaving these out of account, however, the one fact upon which there is fairly general agreement is that here the apostle sets out in the plainest terms the doctrine of Christ's pre-existence. Christ dwelt within the infinite glory, but He took a human life and went to the depths of humiliation. The contrast between what He was and what He chose to become is immense. The importance of the statement is highlighted when it is remembered that Paul was not intending to issue a formal doctrinal declaration of Christ's prior existence. It appears almost incidentally, in the midst of what is virtually an ethical sermon. Paul wants to illustrate the vast love that Christ demonstrated in descending to our level and below, so that believers might be like-minded and act with humility towards one another. By referring incidentally to the glory that belonged to Christ before His entering human life, Paul is making clear that the truth was well known his readers. It was an integral part of the gospel he had preached to them.

Apart from these two important passages, there are other statements that must also be read as alluding to our Lord's pre-existence. 2 Corinthians 8:9, for example, contrasts the riches He surrendered when He temporally abdicated the throne and the poverty He assumed when He entered our human condition. Verses such as Romans 8:3, 1 Corinthians 10:4 and Galatians 4:4 also refer to the actual and personal existence of the Son of God before His appearance within history.

It is not possible to explain away such statements by saying that they mean no more than that Christ existed merely as an idea in the mind of God; that He existed, that is, only in the divine foreknowledge, but not as a divine reality. No such exegesis can be true to the passages themselves; nor can it do justice to the whole New Testament understanding of the Son of God who came to be the Redeemer of humanity. Equally impossible is the suggestion that Paul was merely taking up into his account of Christ Jewish notions of the ideal pre-existence of the Law and the Temple. True enough, the Jews did speak of the ideal existence of these things, but they had not, and could not, have cherished the idea of an actual personal pre-existent Messiah. Nor can it be maintained that the thought of pre-existence came to Paul through the Philonic theory of an ideal or heavenly human, called by Philo "the first man". Paul refers in 1 Corinthians 15:44-49 to "the second man", while the context of the passage shows that it is the exalted Christ, not the pre-existence of Christ, that is here in view.

The idea of our Lord's pre-existence does not lack support outside the definite statements of John's Gospel and the Pauline writings. It is presented clearly in other New Testament books. The opening verses of the letter to the Hebrews imply that the Sonship of Christ goes back beyond the time when He shared flesh and blood. His origin was in God and as God before time, and before His work of atonement on earth and His ministry in heaven. From what we have seen of the Christology of Revelation Christ's pre-existence has the strongest support there.

The Son of God

On only a few occasions in the Synoptic Gospels does Jesus designate Himself Son of God. Thirty-two times, however, He is called by this name by others, and He sometimes adopts the title or accepts it in a form appropriate to Himself. He often speaks of God as His Father in such a way as to reveal a profound and unique relationship to God. Several times He or the Gospel writers use the term "Son" with a prefix that underscores His special union with God His Father: "the Son", "his Son", "my Son", "my beloved Son" and so on. Apart from these particular references, in some of the parables the title is implied. In the parable of the vineyard the "beloved son" who as the "heir" is cast out and killed clearly stands for Jesus Himself (Matthew 21:38). Less clear, perhaps, is the implication of Jesus' Sonship in the parable of the marriage feast (Matthew 22:2ff.). More significant, however, than the mere numerical occurrence of the titles relating to His Sonship is the basic fact that His work for humans is made to rest throughout the whole New Testament upon the special and personal relation between Him as Son and God as Father. Thus even in the Synoptics the title is meant to convey the existence of a deep kinship between God and Christ.

The term "Son of God" was, of course, well known in Jewish circles. In the Old Testament it is applied to angels (Job 38:7; cp. 1:6; 2:1), to magistrates (Psalm 82:6, 7), to the nation of Israel (Exodus 4:22ff.) and to the theocratic king (2 Samuel 7:14; Psalm 89:27). In the New Testament it is used for the first human (Luke 3:38) and for believers (John 1:12; 1 John 3:1).

All these examples, however, show that the undergirding idea is that of a special nearness to God, of special privileges and endowments conferred by Him. We probably find the origin of the messianic usage in the reference to Jewish kings. The application of the title to the nation culminated in its use for the kings, while in its turn the application of it to the kings found its fulfilment in Him who summed up in Himself the concept of kingship in Israel. But although this political messianic idea is basic to the term, it does not provide its ultimate sense as applied to Christ. All the passages in the Synoptics and John's Gospel point rather to the personal qualities of the one who bears the title and to His unique relationship to the God whose Son He is said to be. The official or messianic sense of the term describes not His essential nature but His office. The Messiah could truly bear the title "Son of God" simply as the heir and representative of God. Yet although the term has a messianic flavour, it is not used as a synonym for "Messiah" in the Gospels and the New Testament generally. Demoniacs may have applied it to Jesus in a messianic sense, and Jesus may have used it as such in His trial before the high priest (Matthew 26:63; cp. verse 68). But in those passages where Jesus speaks of Himself as "the Son" and calls God His "Father", the official messianic idea is entirely absent. He is not, that is to say, called "Son of God" because He is Messiah; He is Messiah because He is Son of God.

Even explanations of the title in terms of an ethical relationship between Jesus and God are not sufficient to express its full significance. Passages such as "My Father, if it is possible..." (Matthew 26:39) and "Father, into your hands..." (Luke 23:46) may be taken to express this personal, ethical relationship, and the profound words of Matthew 11:27 may be seen as its climax. These words (more typical of John's Gospel) are not however a passing emotion in the self-consciousness of Jesus; they flow from His settled conviction and habitual mood. They presuppose a relationship of absolute intimacy.

The ethical relationship demands a deeper one. Thus the title "Son of God" is not an official designation, and "sonship" is not a euphemism for discipleship. Jesus never became a Son; He unfailingly spoke of God as "my Father" and "your Father" but never as "our Father" so as thereby to include Himself with others. To say that the name "Son" means nothing more than the knowledge of God is far from the truth. In the mind of Jesus the unclouded consciousness of an eternally unshared Sonship is the supreme reality. The ethical union implies a metaphysical one, a union of nature. Christ spoke of God as Father and Himself as Son so naturally as to indicate His moral perfection. Thus to say that Jesus was in an ethical relationship to God is to say that He was also in an essential relationship to Him. The consciousness of His own sinlessness gives Him the right to use the title without distortion, and thus to set Him apart from others. Between Jesus and God, indeed, all things are common. It is

Jesus' filial consciousness, not His messianic consciousness, that is the basic fact of the Christian faith and gospel.

In John's Gospel the presentation of the Sonship of Christ has a larger place than in the Synoptics. But the essential facts are still the same. Here we find Jesus calling for faith in Himself as the Son of God (John 10:34-38), and manifestly accepting the use of the title for Himself (11:27). It was for the purpose of establishing this faith in Him as Son of God that the Gospel itself was written (20:31).

A new thought, however, is John's description of the Son as "only-begotten". The word used in 1:14, 18; 3:16, 18 (cp. 1 John 4:9) for "only-begotten" (*monogenēs*) underlines the fact that His Sonship is unique. The thought is centred in the personal being of the Son and not in His generation. Christ is the one, only Son, the one to whom the title belongs in a unique sense, and that distinguishes Him from the many children of God (1:12ff.). In contrast with others He is the only Son, the Son that never was, is, or shall be anything less. In the Septuagint the word *monogenēs* is used to translate the Hebrew word for "only" (*jachid*, e.g. Judges 11:34); and the only begotten one is the only beloved one (Genesis 22:2, 12, 16, where the Septuagint has *agapētos*, "beloved", for "only"; cp. Mark 12:6).

In his letters John speaks of the Son with the same overtones. As Son He was sent by the Father (1 John 4:9, 10, 14), and to Him the Father bears witness (1 John 5:9ff). He is the true object of faith (1 John 5:5, 10, 13) whose blood cleanses from sin (1 John 1:7). He is revealed to undo the works of the devil (1 John 3:8; cp. 3:5), and must be confessed (1 John 4:15) or denied (1 John 2:23). With the Father He bestows grace, mercy and peace (2 John 3).

As we have seen, the Pauline letters and the letter to the Hebrews use the title "Son" or "Son of God" in such a way as to make clear that their authors regarded Him as being perfectly at one with God in His ultimate nature.

We have drawn attention to the fact that the only begotten one is the beloved one. In such passages as Matthew 3:17, Mark 1:11

and Matthew 17:5 *agapētos* appears to be a separate title. Christ is the beloved of the Father. The designation was a current messianic one that united two Old Testament statements: Psalm 2:7, "You are my son; today I have become your father", and Isaiah 42:1, "Here is my servant, whom I uphold, my chosen one in whom I delight". The title "the beloved" in turn appears to be practically synonymous with the "chosen" or "elect" one of Yahweh (Matthew 12:18; Luke 23:35). Paul in Colossians 1:13 speaks of the kingdom of God's beloved Son (or the Son of His love). In so describing Him the apostle is simply reinforcing the special and unique relationship between God and Christ.

The Word of God

The idea of Christ as the "Logos" or Word of God is unique to the Fourth Gospel (1:1-18) among the New Testament books. But it is implied in some measure in other places (Colossians 1:15-18; Hebrews 1:2-4; Revelation 9:13). The Old Testament uses "the word" to denote creative action (Psalm 33:6). The term also occurs frequently in the works of the Jewish-Alexandrian philosopher Philo, a younger contemporary of John's. Scholars debate whether and how far the apostle's teaching was influenced by Logos-ideas current at the time. This is a question which need not concern us here, for the genesis of the Logos doctrine is far less important than its application. We can be sure, however, that the Prologue is an integral part of John's Gospel, and although the term does not find a place in the body of the book its meaning appears everywhere. More specifically, the particular significance of the Logos doctrine reappears under the categories of truth, light and life, which are recurring themes throughout. The designation "truth" describes the nature of the Logos. The connotation of the term is "reality", and for the apostle, it is only in the person of Christ the incarnate Logos that we can take hold of the divine reality.

The word "light" may be said to describe the source of the Logos. Light is a popular symbol of all that is divine and holy. Thus the Logos has come as a Light into the world, from Him who dwells in light that is unapproachable except through Him.

The designation "life" describes the action of the Logos. As Christ, the incarnate Word, He communicates eternal life to those who receive and believe in Him. This is truly life, because it possesses a divine quality.

The Fourth Gospel opens by presenting the Logos in a threefold relationship: first, to God (1:1). In the briefest possible way John emphasises the eternity of the Word: "In the beginning was the Word". John does not say that the Word had a beginning; he is asserting that when there was a beginning the Word was there. The existence of the Word is thus necessarily extended beyond the limits of time. He also makes clear here that the Word has a separate personality: "and the Word was with God", or literally, "towards" (*pros*) God, in fellowship with Him. John also stresses the deity of the Word: "and the Word was God". The term "God" cannot plausibly be given a different connotation here from that of its use immediately before. The Word is not "a god" (with an indefinite article and a small "g") in contrast to "the God" (with the definite article and a capital "G"). The Arians and their modern successors the Jehovah's Witnesses find no support here for their created deity, their honorary god.

This verse is the basis of the whole Gospel. In itself it precludes the false notion that the Word *became* personal, either at the creation or at the incarnation. The eternal relations of the persons of the Godhead furnish the basis for the revelation made in Christ. Precisely because the Word was personally distinct from God, and is yet essentially God, He could make God known; for to repeat, only through God is God known. The three great clauses in which the essential nature of the Word is declared relate to time, mode of being, and character, and reflect the three elements of the incarnation of the Word expressed in John 1:14: He who was God became flesh; He who was with God dwelt among us; He who was in the beginning became (or came to be) in time. John also relates the Word to creation. The existence of the world is the result of His creative activity. Through Him all things were made. He came into the world as the light which gives light to everyone. But He came in a personal form as the Word made flesh. In this world of His own making He showed Himself as light and as an incarnate person. Finally, John relates the Word to personal experience. He came to His own world, but those who were His own people did not receive Him. But to those who did receive Him He gave the right to be called children of God.

John is, therefore, not making a small statement in his reference to Christ as the Word. He is, in fact, making use of a term that expressed the nature of Christ as absolutely divine. In Him, as the Word made flesh, the eternal, self-revealing God was incarnate.

Christ and Lord

With the exception of His birth name, "Jesus", no other has rooted itself so firmly in the thought of the world as that of "Christ". This name is the Greek equivalent of the Hebrew "Messiah", which is rendered into English as "Anointed". Originally it was a title, but soon it became a name and the article was dropped. It came to be combined with the name "Jesus" in the forms "Jesus Christ" or "Christ Jesus", and both Matthew and Mark announce that they are presenting the record of "Jesus Christ".

On a number of occasions Jesus refers to Himself as the Christ. Matthew has some nine references, Mark five and Luke nine. On 24 occasions in the Synoptics others refer to Him as the Christ; some of these are, of course, parallel accounts. In John's Gospel, too, the name appears frequently, but here its titular significance is stressed several times, as in 1:41, where the identity of Jesus with the expected Messiah is made clear.

In the Old Testament the king was referred to as the Lord's "anointed" (Psalm 18:50) in virtue of the pouring upon him of the sacred oil, which was a symbol of the Spirit of God. Out of the failure of the kings, reinforced by the prophetic word, grew the expectation of the coming ideal King who would fulfil the hopes of Israel. It is this ideal figure who is pictured in Isaiah 11:1-5. In Psalm 2 the title "Messiah" (Anointed) is attached to this expected figure, and as the hope of the appearance of the coming deliverer grew stronger in Israel the title "the Messiah" was increasingly applied to Him. So it was that in the heyday of the Baptist's ministry, "The people were waiting expectantly and were all wondering in their hearts if John might possibly be the Messiah" (Luke 3:15). It is not surprising that Jesus should rebuke the devils for proclaiming the fact that He was the Christ. This was possibly because of the colourful Jewish notion that their coming king would be a warrior with pomp and power, and because He wanted those who would follow Him to make the discovery for themselves. At the same time there were vital moments in His life when Jesus declared that He was the expected Messiah.

For example, in the synagogue of Nazareth (Luke 4:18, 19) He took to Himself the prophetic words of Isaiah 61:1-2. The word "anointed" in the passage that He claimed to fulfil must have suggested the "Anointed One". This particular Scripture is significant, since it reveals not the awaited Messiah of the national Jewish kind, but a "Servant of the Lord" whose mission was to bring spiritual enlightenment and salvation to the poor. In Matthew 11:3 the question of the Baptist and our Lord's reply implicitly but clearly refer to the Messiah. In the crisis at Caesarea Philippi (Matthew 16:16) Jesus drew from His disciples the acknowledgement that He was the Christ, and He rejoiced openly in their testimony. He had secured the confession of His Messiahship; now those disciples were to learn what kind of Messiah He was (cp. Matthew 16:21). Then at His trial He was asked a direct question regarding His messianic claims, and having been put on solemn oath by the priests He declared that He was indeed the Christ (Matthew 26:63ff.). Jesus was crucified because He confessed His Messiahship. Matthew 26:63ff. unites the three titles, "Messiah", "Son of Man" and "Son of the Blessed". For the believers of the primitive Church, then, the Jesus whom they revered and worshipped was truly the Christ, the Messiah of God.

In the Old Testament, however, not only the king was anointed, but also the priest. In fact, in some passages the High Priest, as distinguished from the ordinary priests, appears to bear the semi-title "the anointed priest" (Leviticus 4:3, 5, 16; 6:22; see also Exodus 28:41; 30:30 etc.). Thus Christ the Messiah is both the regal Priest and the priestly King. As we move on into the rest of the New Testament we find that *Christos* is now a proper name, since its messianic significance expressed in the title "the Messiah", "the Christ", is less meaningful to the growing Gentile churches. But the essential facts of His kingship and priesthood remain, and the name itself becomes associated with others such as "Son of God" and "Lord". In such associations it acquires an even deeper meaning. It would seem, indeed, that what was regarded as most important about Christ was not the office He held but the person He was. It was this that gave meaning to His work for us. He is, therefore, as Paul says (using the fullest of His titles), "our Lord Jesus Christ".

Like the term "Christ", that of "Lord" acquires a deeper meaning in the New Testament. The Greek word *kyrios*, either with or without the article, occurs over 240 times in the Gospels. This large number of instances is, however, obscured by the fact that many English words are used as equivalents; for example, it is sometimes translated "master" or "lord" (Matthew 15:27), sometimes "Sir" (Matthew 21:30), sometimes "owner" (Luke 19:33). The fundamental significance of the term is that it describes one who has power or authority over persons or things. It implies ownership and thus is used as a title of courtesy or reverence. In many places it is addressed to Jesus in this way or is used as a name for Him. His disciples use it without the article: "'Lord, if it's you,' Peter replied, 'tell me to come to you on the water'" (Matthew 14:28). It is, as is to be expected, more frequent in the Fourth Gospel, since this records in fuller detail the private discussions between Jesus and His disciples. Jesus also applied it to Himself (Matthew 7:21), and it is given to Him by the angels (Luke 2:11).

Without the article, then, the word appears as a name. But it also occurs in many instances with the article as a title. In this sense Christ applies it to Himself (John 13:13). This use of the title is found most frequently in Luke (18 times) and John (12 times). Most of John's instances are found in the last two chapters of the Gospel and in passages peculiar to him. They deal with Christ's risen life and were written at a time when a higher conception of His person was giving a deeper significance to the title, and when its confessional meaning was fully known. The adoring cry of Thomas (John 20:28) illustrates how, among Jewish Christians, a title of respect addressed to a teacher had become one of divine honour. Within the Gospels themselves the disciples' respect for their teacher becomes a realisation that He is more (Luke 5:8). To the Jewish Christian Jesus was "Messiah"; to the Hellenistic Christian Jew He was "the Christ"; to the Gentile Christian He was "the Lord". And all three are combined in the familiar name "the Lord Jesus Christ". The Christ is the Lord, the possessor and ruler of the kingdom of God.

In the rest of the New Testament the title "Lord" is frequent, being found some 46 times in the epistles. Throughout the idea of sovereignty is maintained (2 Corinthians 10:8; 1 Thessalonians 4:16; 1 Corinthians 5:4-5; 1 Thessalonians 4:1, 2, 6; Romans 14:9; 10:12; Philippians 2:11). Thus we note that the title "Lord", which seems to have been a general title of respect, bursts its limits in the New Testament in being applied to Jesus' special relationship to God, and so became a confession of His superhuman nature and of His deity.

THE REDEEMING REALITY

"How can you say,
'The Son of Man
must be lifted up'?"

Chapter 6

∽

The Nature of Christ's Work

Christians frequently express their gratitude to God the Father for giving His Son, but far too seldom do we express gratitude to the Son for giving us the Father. From one point of view this is precisely what Christ has done. "No one comes to the Father except through me" (John 14:6). In the Son we encounter the Father (John 8:19; 14:8 etc.). There is no other way of meeting God as Father except in the one who is declared to be Son of God. It is in His Sonship that people become children of God; in relationship with Him we can speak confidently of God in terms of "Abba, Father" (Romans 8:15; Galatians 4:6). In and through His unbroken Sonship humanity's broken sonship is restored.

Christ is not, however, a model of the noblest human endeavours. He did not come to stimulate our struggling consciousness of God; He came to deal with our deeper consciousness of sin. His purpose in the world is not to inspire people at their best but to redeem people at their worst. And to do that He must take account of human sin, the real barrier in the way of our approach to God. It is the very heart of the gospel that in and through Christ the way is opened up for humanity to re-establish our relationship with God, broken as a result of our sinful rebellion. What humans supremely need, therefore, is to hear the good news about God, the declaration that in Christ God has taken action on their behalf.

All this puts Christ in a special position. It makes Him the Mediator, not the medium, of the holy grace of God. He is the Revealer, and in no way the rival of God. He is the Redeemer, and not just the champion, or even the example, of humankind. As Son of God He has brought and bought salvation, as only the Son of God could or would do. He is the divine forgiveness made incarnate and available for us. He comes as one who actually redeems and does not merely offer redemption; as the divine destroyer of the guilt of sin; as the eternal salvation of God made personally visible in history. Jesus did not come to give us a gospel; He came to be the Gospel. The good news is that a Saviour has come, born to die, "born to raise the sons of earth, born to give them second birth". This makes Jesus different. His work puts Him in a category of His own. He is not simply the greatest of the prophets, or the noblest of spiritual heroes, or the wisest of humanity's seers, or the holiest of its saints. The truth is rather that Calvary is the very throne of God, and the Christ who suffered there was no martyr.

There is much that could be said here, but we will emphasise just two important areas.

The Unity of Christ's Person and Work

Christ's presence in the world is nothing less than the redeeming revelation of God. The subject of Christ's person cannot rightly be kept separate from His work. False views can easily arise if either is subordinated to the other: His person to His work or His work to His person.

When Christ's work is seen as more important than His person, a merely subjective or functional view of the person may result. For some theologians Christ is little more than the sum of one's religious feelings, the archetype of the religious person, who differs from us only in the extent of His natural consciousness of God. His work is to stimulate our dormant consciousness of God rather than to save us from our awakening consciousness of sin. Others conceive the "Godhead" of Jesus as little more than the expression of His value for the religious thought of the believer. They rob our Lord's deity of any objectivity. Christ does no more than model and enable our appreciation of God. His pre-eminence over others is purely historical, not essential. The "deity" of Christ is only another way of saying that Jesus is superior to all other humans as the founder of a spiritual and ethical kingdom.

On the other hand, if Christ's work is subordinated to His person, the result can be equally disastrous and unbiblical. In this case faith can become altogether speculative. The person of Christ is discussed apart from His saving work. At one extreme, some have reduced Him to a mere teacher of ethical precepts; at the other, some have ended up by paying Christ "metaphysical compliments", but without experiencing the work He accomplished.

The right balance is to keep the work and the person of Christ together, as one indissoluble unity. The events that centre on the action of Christ and on His person are the subject-matter of Christianity. Throughout the ages both who Christ is and what He has done and does have been understood as the revealed truth, proclaimed as the essential gospel, experienced as redemption and sung about with grateful wonder. It was the custom of the early Church Fathers to underscore the words "is" and "am" in such declarations as "He is the Word", "I am the door" and "I am the good Shepherd". In this way they sought to emphasise the unity of the person and the work of Christ. The one who is the door by whom we enter to find salvation, and the one who as shepherd gave His life for the sheep, is the 'I am'. The unity of Christ's person and work is characteristic of Christian faith and experience.

Here is one example from a report written at the time of the Welsh revival in 1904: "The whole revival is marvellously characterised by a confession of Jesus Christ, giving testimony to His power to save, His goodness and His beneficence, and the testimony merging repeatedly into outbursts of singing". This is the authentic biblical note: the confession of Jesus Christ and testimony to His power to save. It is precisely by being Himself that Jesus has done for humans what no other human could do and made divinely available to every human what all humans need.

The Uniqueness of the Work of the Person

"'You are to give him the name Jesus, because He will save his people from their sins'" (Matthew 1:21). Christ's own understanding of Himself was that as Son of Man He had come to seek and to save what was lost (Luke 19:10). It is one of the "trustworthy sayings" of Gospel faith that Christ Jesus came into the world to save sinners (1 Timothy 1:15). "To save", then, describes the mission of Jesus in the world. Yet, as we shall see when we discuss the title "Saviour" below, the name "Saviour" occurs only twice in the Synoptic Gospels. But the title implies what He was and is in His very nature (Luke 2:11; cp. 1:47). He impressed upon His contemporaries that this was the purpose of His presence among them. The idea was almost forced on those who had no experience themselves of His saving activity. "He saved others", it was said at the cross, and this sneer indicated that the conception of Christ as Saviour was widespread. There are five uses in Luke's Gospel of the word "salvation" (1:69, 77; 2:30; 3:6; 19:9), and in each case it refers directly to Christ. In some passages it is almost personified into a title for Jesus. The Holy Spirit revealed to the godly Simeon, who was waiting for the consolation of Israel, that the child brought into the temple was "the Lord's Christ" (Luke 2:25-26). Taking Him in his arms, he thanked God that his eyes had seen God's salvation (verse 30; cp. 3:6). In accepting the invitation of Zacchaeus, Jesus declared that in His coming to him, salvation had entered his house (Luke 19:9).

In the book of Acts the term "salvation" appears six times. The concept is frequently used in the epistles, as we should expect in view

THE NATURE OF CHRIST'S WORK

of their purpose to instruct believers in the facts and implications of their experience of grace. It is found 32 times, 35 if Revelation is included.

In view of the fact that the idea of "saving" occurs most often in connection with Christ's healing miracles, the curative connotation of the term would be uppermost in the popular mind (Matthew 9:22, par. Mark 5:34; Luke 8:48; Matthew 27:42, par. Mark 15:31; Luke 23:35; Mark 3:4, par. Luke 6:9; Mark 5:23; 6:56; 10:52; Luke 7:50; 8:36, 50; 17:19; 18:42). In Jewish thinking coloured by the Old Testament understanding of salvation, "saving" was synonymous with healing.

But there are passages where the curative idea is not present (see, for example, Matthew 8:25; 14:30; 24:22; 27:49). In other places a more "spiritual" connotation of the term is required (for example Mark 8:35, par. Luke 9:24; cp. Matthew 16:25; Matthew 10:22; 24:13; Mark 13:13).

An important passage illustrating the fuller meaning of Christ's saving mission is the story of the rich young ruler (Matthew 19:23ff.). Here it is shown that to "be saved" (verse 25), to "enter into the kingdom of God" (verse 24) and to "inherit eternal life" (verse 29), are three ways of saying the same thing.

The greater idea in the background is that of transference out of the sphere of death into life. More particularly, Christ's saving work is seen as a spiritual deliverance of people from sin and the imparting of new life, fitting them for the kingdom of God, which has begun now as the rule of God in their hearts.

This is the salvation of God through God's saving act in Christ. But central to the whole idea of salvation is that of forgiveness (Ephesians 1:7; cp. 4:32; see Acts 5:31; 13:38; 26:18 etc.). The really new thing in the gospel is this: that Christ did not, like the teachers before Him, declare forgiveness as a general truth (Psalm 86:5); He granted it as a fact in His own name and by His own authority. No prophet from Israel's past ever dared to take this honour on himself or herself. Jesus embodied in Himself the forgiveness of God.

The incident of the paralysed man (Matthew 9:2-8; Mark 2:1-12; Luke 5:17-26) evidently made a deep impression in this respect, since it is recorded that the people were astonished, praised God and acknowledged that a power belonging properly and only to God had been demonstrated by this man, Jesus (see Luke 7:36ff.).

But if the forgiving act of Christ is the centre of the salvation of God, then the atoning act of Christ is the basis of it. The clear biblical fact is that where there is no atonement there is no gospel. The simplest of all gospel truths, which is also the deepest of all theological ideas, is that He bore our sins. Scripture is focused on the doctrine of the atonement. Here is to be found its dynamic centre, which makes it a gospel for humanity. The assertion that God is love has no meaning apart from the work of Christ; God so loved the world that He gave His only Son. Even to talk of the love of Christ without reference to His Cross is to speak vaguely. The biblical way of declaring Christ's love is that He "loved me and gave himself for me". Only in the cross are both the love of God and the love of Christ revealed, realised and made effective for salvation.

But as the new element in Christ's teaching was the assertion of the right, and the proof of the fact, that He could forgive sins, the decisive element of His atoning work is its relation to forgiveness. To preach the love of God without relating it to sin or to the death of Christ, or to preach the forgiveness of sins as the free gift of God's love while assigning no special significance to the death of Christ, is not to preach the New Testament Gospel at all.

It is only a cross-centred Gospel that takes human sin and need seriously. It is through faith in the Christ who has done this atoning work that we are reconciled. Through the cross we receive justification. To proclaim redemption or forgiveness without atonement is to conceive of sin as something natural, like sickness, as nothing worse than error. It is in the Christ of the cross that God speaks His word of pardon and declares our acceptance in His Son.

Some suggest that it is the teaching of Jesus that is of saving value, and that adherence to His words is the way of salvation. He certainly declared that His words are spirit and life (John 6:63). But He clearly did not intend to divorce His words from Himself. His words gain their life from His life and their spirit from His Spirit. They have their value only because they are His words. They find their authority in Him. We cannot separate what He said from who He is. Ultimately to receive His words is to receive Him; and to receive Him with His words is to receive our greatest need, His word of forgiveness through His cross. He came to bring people to the kingdom of God, that through Him they might be forgiven and have eternal life. But He has to suffer and die. He must be "lifted up" on Golgotha's cross. According to His own teaching, His suffering and dying have some vital connection with the purpose of His coming.

Without doubt the cross was present in Christ's filial and messianic consciousness from the beginning. But it was after the great confession of Peter at Caesarea Philippi that He proclaimed it. All three Synoptics introduce our Lord's explicit teaching concerning His death at this point (Matthew 16:21; Mark 8:31; Luke 9:22). His audience was now not so much the crowds as the Twelve; His method was not so much preaching as teaching; His subject was not so much the Kingdom as Himself and in particular His death. He makes it clear that the way of the cross is the way appointed for the Lord's anointed, if He is to accomplish His work. He must die, not by any external necessity, but because of an internal necessity relating to the fulfilment of His divine mission. He has come to seek and to save what was lost, and to do this He must be arrested and then crucified and slain by wicked people.

Between His death and His saving work there is, then, a vital connection: it is in this way that we may enter the kingdom as forgiven sinners. He gives His life as a "ransom for many" (Matthew 20:28; Mark 10:45). It is by His surrendered life that the forfeited lives of humans are liberated. And the blood of His cross will establish a new covenant (Mark 14:22-24). His blood has sacrificial and propitiatory power. In His death there is salvation for humans; this is Christ's own understanding of His work (John 3:16; 6:51-53; 10:11, 28; 12:27-33; 15:13). As Son, Christ came to do the will of the Father; and obedience to that will, for the sake of human salvation, brought Him to the cross. Whatever we owe as pardoned sinners to the love and mercy of God we owe to the death of Christ.

Of course, a fuller statement of the meaning of the cross could be made only after the crowning event itself had taken place. It is no wonder, therefore, that the cross looms large in the inspired interpretation of Christ's person and work. For Paul and the other New Testament writers, the doctrine of Christ's death was not a theology, but the Gospel. And it is interpreted in a variety of ways, but always in relation to the full salvation of humanity. It is related to the divine love (Romans 5:7ff.; 2 Corinthians 5:14; Ephesians 5:25), to law (Galatians 3:13) and to human sin (1 Corinthians 15:3; Galatians 1:4; Ephesians 1:7; Colossians 1:14; Hebrews 9:28; 1 Peter 3:18). It is viewed as substitution (Romans 4:25; Galatians 1:4; 1 Thessalonians 5:10 etc.), as redemption (Galatians 3:14; 4:4; Ephesians 1:7; Colossians 1:13 etc.), as propitiation (Romans 3:24-26 etc.) and as reconciliation (Romans 5:10, 11 etc.).

Numerous metaphors are used to provide some understanding of what Christ accomplished on the cross. There is more in the cross than can ever be put into words. So great is our salvation that the principle is seen to be true: "not by one way only can we reach so great a secret".

The red thread of salvation through the blood of Christ, the Son of God, is woven into all allusions to His saving work. The greatness, the glory and the grace of the divine Christ shine forth everywhere. It is He and He alone who could do, and did, this great thing for us. It is at the cross that He is understood. How can you say that the Son of Man must be lifted up? Why the cross? The cross assures us of His greatness: "'When you have lifted up the Son of Man, then you will know that I am he'" (John 8:28). The cross persuades us of His glory: "And I, when I am lifted up from the earth, will draw all people to myself'" (John 12:32). The cross is the measure of His grace: "'Just as Moses lifted up the snake in the wilderness, so the Son of Man must be lifted up'" (John 3:14). His cross is assurance, attraction and atonement.

The saving work of God is, then, the atoning work of Christ; and the reconciling work of the Father is the saving work of the Son. By His cross and passion, in gracious fulfilment of the loving purpose of the Father, Jesus Christ the Son of God has once and for all, on behalf of and instead of sinful people, made a full and perfect atonement for the sins of the world, by which the broken relation of humans to God is restored and the barrier to communion with God removed.

A study of what God has done in Christ and what Christ has done for us before God can only make forgiven people want to add their voices to those who gladly sing, "'Salvation belongs to our God, who sits on the throne, and to the Lamb'" (Revelation 7:10).

Chapter 7

⚜

The Names of the Worker

The Lamb of God

It is to the "testimony of John", the witness in the wilderness, that we owe the great declaration that Christ is the Lamb of God who takes away the sins of the world. A very good case could be made for the thesis that in this John, son of Zechariah, we have the first and most impressive teacher of theology, the one who has given us the first and most impressive conception of Jesus Christ. John was certainly the first to identify the One who came to him to be baptised as gathering up in Himself all the strands of ancient prophecy and ritual in the religion of Israel relating to the lamb. In contrast with the successive statements and sacrifices of the Old Testament, in which a lamb of the flock has a central place, He is said to be the Lamb of God. As such He takes away the sin of the world. The Lamb of God: there is a whole theology in the title.

Some have suggested that the background to the Baptist's declaration is the Passover lamb of Exodus 12:3ff.; others locate it in the sacrificial lamb of Isaiah 53:7. In favour of the first is the fact that Jewish festivals appear to have had a special interest for the writer of the Gospel. Against it, however, is the fact that the Passover lamb had no specific reference to sin. But it should be noted that the blood of the lamb in Exodus was the sign and seal of salvation (Exodus 12; 1 Corinthians 5:7; 1 Peter 1:18, 19). The second suggestion is especially appealing because the word *amnos* is used in both the Septuagint of Isaiah and John the Baptist's declaration. John, like the eunuch on a later occasion, seems to have been meditating particularly on the prophecy of Isaiah, since he quotes from chapter 40 the day before.

Others, noting the tenderness of the lamb to whom reference is made in Jeremiah 11:19, "I had been like a gentle lamb led to the slaughter," consider this to have been the source of the Baptist's affirmation concerning Jesus. The passage concerning the ritual of the lamb slain at the morning and evening sacrifice (Exodus 29:38-46) is thought by some commentators to be the more likely background of the words of John.

Perhaps too much effort has been expended in seeking to link John's declaration with a limited or specific Old Testament passage. A lamb relating to the sin, the need, and the worship of the people has a particularly significant place in the progressive revelation of God's saving purpose in the Old Testament. It runs right through the whole, unfolding record of the history of salvation. If Exodus tells us of the necessity of the lamb, then Leviticus may be said to specify the purity of the lamb: it must be a lamb without blemish. Isaiah points to the personality of the lamb: He is brought as a lamb to the slaughter. But it was left to John the Baptist, the last of the prophets, to affirm the identity of the Lamb.

Fundamental to the use of the term in the context of God's gracious purpose for humanity is the idea of sacrifice. For the Baptist the one who had come to him to be baptised with the baptism for repentance was in so doing identifying Himself with human sin. It was disclosed to John that He must be the Lamb of God, upon whom the Lord was laying the sins of the world.

From the beginning, the Lamb of God is seen to be one and the same with the Messiah who was to come (cf. John 1:29, 36, 41). The expected Messiah was a very worthy person. Could it be that John's spiritual knowledge had gone deeper than we have hitherto supposed and that it was as a result of his not obviously seeing this glory that he found himself giving way to passing doubt (Matthew 11:2ff.)?

In the year that King Uzziah died the prophet of Israel saw the Lord high and lifted up, majestic and glorious. That was his first dazzling vision. Then as he waited and watched he saw again, one like a Lamb brought to the slaughter. First looks are not always conclusive. We have to go deeper and to look longer if we are to get to the full truth. Isaiah saw the Lord and Isaiah saw the Lamb. Did he identify them for himself? We do not know. John the Baptist certainly did. He saw the Lamb as the Lord, and the Lord as the Lamb. He told his followers to see Him as the Lamb of God who takes away the sin of the world. In one great act of faith he saw the excellence of the Lamb's person: He is the Lamb of God. And he saw the efficacy of the Lamb's sacrifice: He takes away the sin of the world. So in this term Jesus' mission is described: He stands in a special relation to God, which includes the expiatory sacrifice of Himself for the sins of the world. It explains the significance of His own coming as described in such passages as John 12:47: "'I did not come to judge the world, but to save the world.'"

The Lamb of God is disclosed prophetically in the whole sacrificial system, culminating in the Passover, and finding its greatest expression in Isaiah 53. In the book of Revelation the work of the Lamb is set in an eternal context (5:6; 13:8). His sacrifice and sovereignty are emphasised here.

The sacrificial significance of the title is either clear (Revelation 5:12; 13:8; cp. 5:6, 9; 7:14) or implied (Revelation 5:8, 13; 6:1, 16 etc.), whether the word used is *amnos* as in John 1:29, 36; Acts 8:32; 1 Peter 1:19, or *arnion* as in Revelation. At the same time it is made very clear that the one who accomplished this sacrificial work for humans is most intimately related to God. His nature is such that what He has done reflects His timelessness (cf. Revelation 5:6; 13:8; Hebrews 9:12, 14; 13:20). In the term "Lamb", or the extended

"Lamb of God" used by the Baptist, the work and the person of Christ are vividly and vitally related. His sacrificial work can be understood only as that of someone both human and divine.

The One Mediator

Although Christ is explicitly referred to as the Messiah on four occasions only, and three of the four instances have the same context (Hebrews 8:6; 9:15; 12:24), the idea of His mediatorship is basic to the whole New Testament, to what Christ is in Himself and what He does for human salvation. It is on the office of mediator that the other offices of the Saviour depend; it is the root of which they are the different branches, the function of which others are only the several component parts.

It is in the title "mediator" that the person and work of Christ most obviously come together. It is His reconciling work of mediation that provides the proper evangelical foundation for a doctrine of the person of Christ. The decisive importance of Christ is that He is the one who can do this for us. As mediator, Jesus stands for God before humans, and for humans before God. His significance is not simply that He was something, but, more specifically, that He did what He did because He was what He was. As mediator Jesus confronts us on God's behalf, and in Him God acts decisively for us. In Him God meets us, since in Him our sin was dealt with in judgment and in mercy. His presence and His work in the world, and for it, are God's greatest gift to us.

In Christ God meets us and we can meet God. God comes to impart divine life through a life and a work that are truly human. God and humanity come together in Jesus Christ, for to effect a real mediation the mediator must be Himself both human and divine. If Jesus had been a shadowy figure only, and not really a human being, He might have conveyed the illusion of being human, but He could not have been the mediator; and if He had been a god in name only, and not really God, He might have been a martyr, but He could not have been the mediator. No inspiration, however noble, and no imparting of grace, however full, could have equipped Him to be the mediator. None of the Old Testament prophets and none of the angelic host could have been the mediator in the highest Biblical sense. Only the one who was from the beginning "in closest relationship with the Father" (John 1:18), and who "became flesh and made his dwelling among us" (John 1:14), can meet the requirements of this role.

His mediatorship is not an office conveyed to Him by grace, nor a place accorded to Him as reward. He bears the title of mediator because He is what it expresses. All the other titles of Christ find their ground and their significance here. It has been suggested that the title "mediator" relates specifically to salvation, but the same might be said for every reference to Christ throughout the New Testament. Even passages that relate particularly to the nature of Christ are important to the writers because of their significance for salvation. Titles that express the character of Christ's saving work have implications for his person, and those that describe his person have implications for salvation.

The Greek word *mesitēs* translated "mediator" in the New Testament, is used in the Greek Old Testament of Job 9:33 and 16:21 to translate the Hebrew word *mokiach*. Job finds himself unsure in the presence of God. He longs for an arbiter, someone who could act as a go-between and mediate between God and Job. The New Testament provides the answer to Job's longing. There is someone who stands between God and humankind, someone who sits on the throne of God as a human being. In Him the human race has its mediator between itself and God.

In the Old Testament Israel had a mediator in Moses, through whom the law was given (Galatians 3:19; cp. John 1:17), and who stood in for his people when they sinned and were in peril (Exodus 32:11ff. etc.). From the days of Philo the title "mediator" was in general use as a designation of Moses, who had represented the people of Israel before God in the crisis days of their history, and more particularly as the one to whom God communicated the words of His covenant.

In two New Testament books the word "mediator" is applied to Christ: in the letter to the Hebrews He is connected to the foundation of the new covenant; in 1 Timothy (2:5), His reconciling activity is emphasised.

Christ is the mediator of the new covenant (Hebrews 8:6; 9:15; 12:24). At the institution of the Last Supper, Jesus referred to the cup as the new covenant in His blood (Matthew 26:28). In Exodus 24, Moses, the mediator of the law, read the words of the covenant and heard the people's promise of obedience, and then sprinkled both the book and the people (Exodus 24:6-8; Hebrews 9:18ff.). In this way he ratified the covenant between God and the assembly of Israel. In a similar way Christ has become the mediator of the new covenant by ratifying it with His own blood, shed for the remission of sins. Thus is Christ revealed, by contrast, as the true mediator of "the new covenant ... established upon better promises" (Hebrews 8:6). His is "a better covenant" (7:22) based upon a better sacrifice (9:23), by reason of the "blood that speaks a better word than the blood of Abel" (12:24). Thus a "better hope" (7:19) is assured to those who are "cleansed" of their sin (9:22), "sanctified" (10:29), and have access by the blood of Jesus (10:19), for "better possessions" (10:34) and "a better country" (11:16). For this reason the mediator of the new covenant is "superior to the angels" (1:4).

In the passage in 1 Timothy, the apostle argues that God, who is the Saviour of all those who believe, wills also the salvation of all people (1 Timothy 2:1-6). The mediator is Himself "God our Saviour". But He took our nature and in that nature offered Himself for the salvation of humankind. This is the special point the apostle wishes to emphasise.

The one who has taken the place of mediator has all the human qualities necessary to discharge His mediatorship. The mediator is really, fully and perfectly human. Yet although this is Paul's main point here, he implies clearly that if He were only human He could not identify Himself with humanity as He has done. He has come to us from beyond the gulf that divides humans from God, from beyond the breach that separates us and that no mere human could span.

As mediator of the new covenant and as the one mediator between God and humans, Jesus has, then, both the divine dignity and the human status necessary for His office. Christologically, therefore, the term "mediator" is of utmost significance. It is the fundamental truth of the gospel that in Christ humanity is united with God. He is the bond between us; in Him mediation is effected and made real. Out of this truth every other truth connected with our great salvation flows; and in this fact every other fact about Jesus Christ the Lord may be found. The humanity through which He is ours, and the deity by which He is God's, are both essential to Him. As mediator He stands alone.

Closely allied with the idea of mediatorship are those of intercessor (Hebrews 7:24, 25; cp. Romans 8:33ff.) and advocate (1 John 2:1). As mediator, Jesus has gained access for us into the presence of God. As intercessor He acts to further our petitions with the Father. As advocate, He answers every charge that sin and the devil can lay against us, and He represents our case and cause in such a way as, at all times, to clear the guilty.

The Saviour of the World

It was the Samaritans who believed for eternal life after Christ's personal appearance among them who, according to John's Gospel, gave to Him the great title of "the Saviour of the world" (John 4:42). It was His own presence as the transformer of human life, following the testimony of the woman He had met by the well, that provoked this profound confession. The Samaritans, more readily than the Jews, would have appreciated the wider significance of Christ's mission. "He had to pass through Samaria," says the evangelist. But this necessity was a matter not of geography but of grace. There was a direct route to Galilee, but Jesus did not take it. He intended to pass through Samaria and thus to visit a mixed race bitterly hated by the

Jews. "Two nations my soul detests," says the apocryphal book of Sirach, "and the third is not even a people: Those who live in Seir, and the Philistines, and the foolish people that live in Shechem." The Samaritans were cursed in the temple and their food reckoned as unclean as the flesh of pigs. It was to such people that Christ came. By the sheer graciousness and glory of His own person He created such an impression that those who saw Him believed in and confessed Him as the longed-for "Saviour of the World".

The term "saviour" (*sotēr*), like that of "mediator", signifies everything that He had come to do as a divine person. He Himself, and after Him the writers of the New Testament, used the term "to save" as a comprehensive description of His mission. The New Testament is punctuated with evidence of the saving action of Christ and with its proclamation. Faith in Christ as Saviour, in the event that took place once and for all in the atoning work of the cross, is the Christian faith. In distinction from all other forms of religion, the Christian Gospel is proclaimed as faith in Jesus Christ as our God and Saviour. The whole New Testament reveals that there is no possibility of everlasting life except through faith in Him, in whom God has come to us to reveal Himself and make known His salvation. Thus the entire Christian faith has a Christological foundation; it is faith in someone in and through whom we have the salvation of God.

But although the idea of salvation is prominent in the New Testament, the formal title "Saviour" is applied to Christ relatively infrequently. It does not occur at all in Matthew or Mark. In Luke it appears twice (1:47; 2:11). The second of these references is to the angels' announcement of Jesus as "a Saviour ... who is the Messiah, the Lord". Without going into detail about how these designations are to be understood, it seems that two lines of prophetic hope were united in the angelic message. The child who was born was connected with the promised coming of Yahweh for the salvation of Israel, and at the same time He fulfilled the predictions of the coming Davidic King. This is the Saviour, both the promised Messiah and the sovereign Lord.

In the other Lucan writing, the Acts of the Apostles, the term occurs in just two passages (5:31; 13:23). Jesus is said in 5:31 to be a "Prince and Saviour" (cp. 3:15, "the author of life; Hebrews 2:10, "the author of their salvation"; the Greek word carries the meaning of "arch-leader"). In 13:23 He is declared to be the Saviour of Israel, and this Saviour is also from the seed of David, yet in the same context He is stated to be the begotten Son of God (verse 33), and the Holy One who saw no decay (verse 31).

Apart from the later Pastoral letters the term appears only twice in Paul's other epistles (Philippians 3:20; Ephesians 5:23), although the saving grace of Christ's person and work is discussed in all the apostle's writings. There is no reason, therefore, to accept the claim that the infrequency of Paul's use of the term implies his deliberate avoidance of the title.

In the Philippian letter, written from prison, Paul declares that "our citizenship is in heaven. And we eagerly await a Saviour from there, the Lord Jesus Christ" (3:20). The apostle is making the point that complete salvation involves the redemption of the body. It is for this that we await the Saviour whose has the power to bring all things under His control. In Ephesians Paul deals with the subject of the mutual relationships between husband and wife, which he considers to be partially parallel to that between Christ and His Church. He declares Christ to be the Saviour of the body, which is the Church He loved and for which He gave Himself (Ephesians 5:23, 25).

It is in the Pastorals and in 2 Peter, however, that the title "Saviour" becomes frequent. Paul introduces himself in 1 Timothy as "an apostle of Christ Jesus by the command of God our Saviour and of Christ Jesus our hope" (1:1). Here the Saviour is specified as being God (cp. 2:3; 4:10; Titus 1:3; 3:4). But the term is given no less definitely to Christ (2 Timothy 2:10; Titus 1:4; 2:13; 3:6). This epithet, used interchangeably of God and of Christ, can mean only that the apostle readily and completely assimilated Christ to God. In this way he provides a background for the interpretation of Titus 2:13, which speaks, in contrast with His first coming in grace, of "the appearing of the glory of our great God and Saviour, Jesus Christ" (cp. 1 Timothy 6:14-16; 2 Timothy 4:1-8). The statement of the Saviour's saving work is reckoned a "trustworthy saying" (1 Timothy 1:15). He gave Himself to redeem us (Titus 2:14), and by His grace we are justified (Titus 3:7). In the day when He appears this Jesus will be revealed for what He is, "the blessed and only Ruler, the King of kings and Lord of lords" (1 Timothy 6:15).

In 2 Peter the title "Saviour" is especially associated with one or more of Christ's other names, while the simple "Jesus" and "Christ", do not occur at all (2 Peter 1:11; 2:20; 3:2, 18). The references to Christ as Saviour become more significant when we recall that in several Old Testament passages Yahweh is specifically declared to be the only Saviour of His people. There is none beside Him (Isaiah 43:11; Hosea 13.4; cf. 1 Samuel 10:19; 14.39; 2 Samuel 22:3; Psalm 7:10; 17:7; 107:20-21; Isaiah 43:3). Yahweh is the Holy One of Israel, its Saviour (Isaiah 45:15, 21; 49:26; 60:16; 63:8; Jeremiah 14:8). To call Jesus Christ "the Saviour" with this Old Testament background in mind is deliberately to transfer a divine title to Him. It can hardly be doubted that when Peter wrote he had in the back of his mind the promise of God to send "a saviour and defender" (Isaiah 19:20), and that the person he designates as "our Lord and Saviour Jesus Christ" (1 Peter 1:11; 2:20; 3:18) and "our God and Saviour Jesus Christ" (1:1) was this person. And the day of the Lord is the day of His appearing.

The title "Saviour", then, does not only say something about what Christ does; it also reveals something of what He is. The word is given to Jesus as a divine title. In non-Christian religions the figure of the Saviour is missing, and Gnostic systems borrowed their idea of the *sotēr* from Christianity. In answer to the question, "What new thing did Jesus bring?" the Church father Irenaeus replied, "He brought what was new in bringing Himself. In bringing Himself He brought the salvation of God."

The Exalted Reality

"'Did not the Messiah have to suffer these things and then enter his glory?'"

Chapter 8

∽

Jesus Christ ... Crowned with Glory

The Enthroned Lord

Having endured the cross to fulfil all prophecy, Jesus Christ has taken His place of sovereignty and honour at the right hand of the majesty on high. It was not possible for death to hold Him (Acts 2:24). He who has life in Himself (John 1:4; 9:5) and whose gracious purpose it is to give life to whoever He chooses, to those who believe (John 3:36; 5:21 etc.), could not Himself be contained in a tomb. He conquered the grave, to bring life and immortality to light through the gospel (2 Timothy 1:10). He lives as victor over humanity's last enemy, death (1 Corinthians 15:26, 54). It is the constant affirmation of the New Testament that Christ is risen (Luke 24:34; John 21:14; 1 Corinthians 15:13ff.).

The essence of the gospel as preached by the early Church is found in 1 Corinthians 15:3, 4. He who died for our sins, the apostle says elsewhere, was raised for our justification (Romans 4:5; cp. 5:18). Only a Christ triumphant over the grave can explain the facts that experience attests and history records. The changed outlook, the renewed zeal, the burning conviction, the missionary success of the early disciples and the expansion and continuance of the Church cannot be explained unless Christ, who was dead, is alive again. If the resurrection were a delusion, a misconception or a trick, then the truth, goodness and love that result from it would have no foundation, and life itself would be a mockery. The most sure fact is that Jesus Christ rose again from the dead.

However, the first Church not only preached the news of the risen Christ; it also asserted no less assuredly the glory of the ascended Lord (cf. Acts. 1:2, 9, 11; 2:33ff.; 3:21ff.; 9:3; 22:6; 26:12; Romans 8:34; Ephesians 1:20; 4:10; Philippians 2:9; 1 Timothy 3:16; Hebrews 4:14; 8:1; 9:12, 24; 10:12; 12:2; 1 Peter 3:22). They knew Him risen and they saw Him ascend (Luke 24:50-53). God highly exalted Him with a name above every name. He had declared before the high priest and the Sanhedrin that He would be given a place at the right hand of power. Now He is there, the enthroned Lord.

It is usual and apparently right to identify Psalm 110 as the immediate Old Testament source of the idea of the ascension of the risen Christ and His sitting at the right hand of God. Our Lord, according to all three Synoptic Gospels, claimed that the opening words of the psalm carried a messianic significance (Matthew 22:44; Mark 12.36; Luke 20:42). It is quoted with the same understanding by the apostles Peter (Acts. 2:34; cp. 1 Peter 3:22) and Paul (1 Corinthians 15:25), and the writer of the letter to the Hebrews (5:4; 6:20; 8:1; 10:12ff.). The practical implications of Christ's enthronement are given a large place in the New Testament epistles, and its significance for salvation is also emphasised (Romans 8:33ff.). This may be summarised as follows: it declares our Lord's return to His heavenly glory; it demonstrates the completeness of His propitiatory sacrifice; and it attests to the permanence of His priestly ministry.

The ascension of Jesus follows, indeed, from His whole career: it is the natural consequence of who He had shown Himself to be in the service He rendered to His Father and the work He did for humans.

From the Christological point of view the ascension places the incarnate Christ within the Godhead. He returned to a place where

He was no stranger. While within the human sphere He was not out of touch with the realm of His pre-incarnate glory; during the days of His earthly life He continued the exercise of His cosmic functions.

Returning, however, to where He was before – to His place on the throne of God – He returned as something more than He was before. He brought back to the right hand of the Majesty on high His glorified humanity. Christ ascended into the heavens, where the Word of God had been before – He was always in the heavens and remained in the Father – but where the Word made flesh had not sat before. As surely as Jesus rose in a real and glorified human body, so He was also raised to heaven in the same body. Paul makes quite evident that He still inhabits a body in glory (Colossians 2:9; Philippians 3:21). When he speaks of the Redeemer, Paul seldom regards Him in any other way than as one who assumed humanity, and in that humanity He is now glorified.

The New Testament never presents the incarnation of Christ as an isolated fact. It is always united organically with the total truth about Him. The writers do not regard Him only as the Word of God incarnate, but also as having enthroned glorified human nature in union with His deity. In the ascension Jesus threw off the restrictions of space – He went from the here to the everywhere – and in the heavenly world human nature reigns in Him. In that nature, glorified in union with the glory of His divinity, is to be found the hope and the goal of redeemed humanity.

On the throne of God Jesus reigns as the glorified Lord. We are called to come boldly to that throne (Hebrews 4:16). There is a king upon that throne; therefore grace is available to us. "You are a king, then!" Pilate said to Him. He is truly a king, but not of this world. The king is all-sufficient for our need. The psalmist says, "The LORD has established his throne in heaven, and his kingdom rules over all" (Psalm 103:19). And there too, in reigning splendour, is the enthroned Lord, to provide His enabling grace to those who need it. There is a human being upon the throne, who can sympathise with our weakness. The carpenter of Nazareth reigns in eternal triumph, but He reigns as a human, as our friend and our brother. There is a priest upon the throne, who represents us before God. The prophet Zechariah saw in his vision a priest on God's throne. Here we have, in the enthroned Saviour, the great high priest, who represents us fully and faithfully before our Father in heaven. There is a Lamb upon the throne, who gives us salvation.

The Enduring Priest

While the idea of Christ as high priest is mentioned elsewhere in Scripture, as in Romans 8:34 and the high priestly prayer of John 17, it is stated most fully in the letter to the Hebrews. Simplifying somewhat, it may be said that the book of Revelation largely comprises a vision of Christ the king and the letter to the Hebrews is our guide to Christ as priest. The title "high priest" is used ten times in the letter (2:17; 3:1; 4:14, 15; 5:5, 10; 6:20; 7:26; 8:1; 9:11), along with "priest" (5:6) and "a great priest" (10:21).

In comparison with the general idea of the coming Messiah as the anointed king, Jewish messianic expectations had little place for the idea of a Christ-priest. It was, however, characteristic of Christianity, in the light thrown on to the promise by its fulfilment, to gather neglected aspects of the Old Testament witness and note their embodiment in Christ. This is particularly true in the case of the letter to the Hebrews, in which the old covenant and the new are related and contrasted. It is especially striking that the writer should find in Psalm 110, which declares the Messiah to be not only David's son but also David's Lord, a reference to Christ's priesthood: "You are a priest for ever, in the order of Melchizedek" (Psalm 110:4; Hebrews 5:6). In the high priesthood of Christ we have everything of lasting worth in the old covenant. The believers to whom this word of exhortation came were being told by their Jewish critics that in following the Nazarene they were losing all the rich splendour of the levitical priesthood. The writer reminds them that far from losing everything, they were really gaining everything in and with this man, who was declared to be the Son of God. Since they have Him as high priest, they have everything that is better and eternal and that cannot be shaken.

At 4:14, the writer starts his discussion of the priesthood of Christ. He begins with a statement about the person of the high priest. Not everyone could be a priest; no one takes the honour upon himself (5:4). So Christ did not glorify (*doxazō*) Himself in being made a high priest (5:5). To Aaron the office was an honour (*timē*). He was authorised to act for God on behalf of the people. But to Christ it was more than an honour, more than an external authority conferred on Him. It was part of the glory that was inseparable from His Sonship. His office springs from His person; it is not, as was the case with Aaron, a prerogative added to His person. His high priesthood was not from humans, and not by the will of the flesh, but from God.

Using the symbol of the historical figure of Melchizedek, the writer emphasises the distinctive feature of our great high priest: his continuing as a priest for ever. Melchizedek was a priest when Abraham met him. His origin and end are unknown. There is no record of his birth or death; he just appeared as a priest. So Jesus is not a priest by physical descent or by legal enactments. He is a priest who is, at the same time, the Son of God; a priest of whom it is said, "Your throne, O God, will last for ever and ever." He always lives; His sympathy and His vocation are unending. He is a priest for ever.

In one central passage, the writer presents Christ's work in relation to His person (9:13-14). The high priest of old brought the blood of bulls and goats. But He "offered Himself". Not just any death can save us; only this one. Here is the fullest sacrifice. The high priests of the ancient priesthood were not without blemish; but He was without sin. Here is the holiest sacrifice. He presents His own blood, a sacrifice of infinite cost. Here is the costliest sacrifice. He offered Himself "through the eternal Spirit". Many able commentators interpret this not as referring to the Holy Spirit, but as stating the nature and spirit of His high priestly offering. Thus the term "spirit" is taken to describe the being or nature of the Son, and "eternal" as an attribute of that nature (cp. 7:3). If this is the way the phrases are to be understood, then they denote the greatest sacrifice.

The writer emphasises what he sees to be the special function of the high priest. He is appointed to deal with matters relating to God. In the writer's view this is Christ's unique function as high priest. And He deals with God on behalf of human sins. The high priest and the blood went together. Because he knows that "every high priest is selected from among the people" (5:1) and is thus appointed to represent the people, he emphasises the humanity of Jesus throughout the epistle, as we have seen. In vital ways, however, the Jewish high priests were unlike our great high priest. His priesthood, unlike theirs, is not mutable and transient. The high priests of the old covenant were subject to weakness; but He was without sin. Our great High Priest has passed into the heavens, where He is enthroned as priest-king. In heaven He lives for us, and He lives there to pray for us.

Although the name "high priest" is connected with the work of Christ, it is no less significant for understanding His person. He is declared to be both human and above the angels, occupying the throne of God. He is human and divine. The ministry that He fulfils brings Him into the closest relationship with us; it is exercised before God, and so is a service that no mere human can offer.

The Expected King

The concept of the kingdom found a large place in the teaching of Jesus. In fact, it is so central and comprehensive that it contains within itself the whole content of the Gospel. The conception was with Jesus all through His ministry. He began His preaching with the announcement that it was near (Matthew 4:17; Mark 1:15), and on the eve of His death He was still speaking of it and anticipating reunion with His disciples there (Mark 14:25).

The idea of the kingdom was familiar to the Jews, and the term was evidently in common usage (1 Chronicles 28:5; Daniel 2:44; 4:3). But the concept was enriched by Jesus. The kingdom was always specifically that "of heaven", or "of God"; and it would seem that Jesus put His emphasis here because in His mind it was something larger, and more spiritual, than the Jewish state. So although Jesus' idea of the kingdom was rooted in the Hebrew Scriptures, it was certainly not confined by them. The more He raised it above popular notions, the more sharply it contrasted with them. The word "kingdom" suggests organisation, association and location. But the term *basileia* instead connotes rule and dominion. The term may be taken as a collective equivalent for "Son of Man", which combines, as we have observed, humility and suffering with apocalyptic triumph in the future. These two senses are also united in the term "kingdom of God" or "of heaven". It has a present and a future reference. It is in process of development now and yet is to be revealed triumphantly in the future. It is the rule of God now in human hearts, but is yet to come in apocalyptic glory. Of course, in every aspect of the kingdom, Jesus is the king. He reigns in the present through grace in the experience of those who have come into the kingdom. He shall reign in the future when He is revealed in power and great glory as king, when every knee shall bow to Him and every tongue shall confess Him as Lord to the glory of God the Father.

The two outstanding features of apocalyptic thought are that the kingdom lies in the future and that it will come suddenly by the actual appearance of God. Throughout the New Testament these two ideas are related to Christ the ascended Lord. He is king upon the throne. In every New Testament letter there is some allusion to the coming of Christ to reign. In Revelation we have a picture of the final victory of God, when the redeemed of all ages sing the song of the Lamb to the one whose works are great and marvellous, the Lord God, the Almighty, whose ways are righteous and true, and who is Himself the king of the ages (15:3). Certainly the conflicts depicted in the book have an historical reference; and every victory of God is itself a judgment of God.

The book depicts the judging act of God both as a series and in its consummation. The judgment as a series of acts is set out in what is undoubtedly the heart of the apocalypse, which begins with the opening of the sealed book in chapter 6 and ends with the pouring out of the bowls in chapter 16. Before the writer recounts the unfolding of impending judgment he unveils the heavenly and eternal background against which coming events will take place (chapters 4 – 5). He sees behind nature and history to reveal their controlling hand, which is the hand of Christ. God has pledged Himself to make an end of evil, and that cannot be done without devastating happenings in a world that is under the control of the evil one. In and through these acts of devastation Christ is manifested as king.

The cycle of judgments leads on to the "last judgment". Throughout Revelation judgment, both present and continuous, and future and final, is unfolded dramatically. In every judgment of God, from first to last, one name stands supreme. He is the Word of God, the King of kings and the Lord of lords. "The kingdom of the world has become the kingdom of our Lord and of His Messiah, and He will reign for ever and ever" (11:15).

The Ultimacy of Jesus Christ

No names for Christ are more expressive than those by which John the seer couples Him with God. He is Alpha and Omega; the First and the Last; the Beginning and the End (Revelation 1:8; 2:8; 21:6; 22:13). In these titles we see the fullness of Christ. He is the fullness of wisdom and knowledge. He is the fullness of space, for all things are in Him and through Him and for Him. He is the fullness of time, for He fills eternity; "before Abraham was born, I am"; He was and is and is to come; He is the same yesterday, today and for ever. Here, too, we see the finality of Christ. There is nothing beyond Him: nothing before, nothing after, nothing more. He has no "before" and no "after". These titles solemnly affirm Christ's eternal deity.

Thus Christ is the Yes and the Amen, authenticating the promises of God (2 Corinthians 1:20). He is also the ruler of God's creation (Revelation 3:14). Jesus Christ is ultimate. Everything of God is to be found in Him.

℘

This man so cured regards the Curer,
then, As – God forgive me ! – who but God Himself,
Creator and Sustainer of the world,
That came and dwelt on it awhile!...
And must have so avouched Himself in fact...
The very God! think, Ahib; dost thou think?

Browning

My Lord and my God ...
Saviour Divine With Glory Crowned

Thou seemest human and divine,
   The highest, holiest, manhood, Thou;
Our wills are ours, we know not how;
   Our wills are ours, to make them Thine!

Tennyson

Bibliography

Athanasius, *On the Incarnation*. Repr. Charleston: BiblioBazaar LLC, 2010.

Karl Barth, *Church Dogmatics*, translated and edited G.W. Bromiley and T.F. Torrance, IV, 1. Edinburgh: T&T Clark, 1956-1975, pp. 157-357.

Richard Bauckham, *Jesus and the God of Israel*. Carlisle: Paternoster, 2008.

G.C. Berkouwer, *The Person of Christ*. Repr. Grand Rapids: Eerdmans, 2000.

Donald G. Bloesch, *Jesus Christ: Savior and Lord*. Downers Grove: InterVarsity Press, 2005.

Darrell Bock, *Jesus according to Scripture*. Grand Rapids and Leicester: Baker Academic and Apollos, 2003.

Robert M. Bowman, Jr. and J. Ed Komoszewski (eds.), *Putting Jesus in His Place*. Grand Rapids: Kregel Publications, 2007.

F.F. Bruce, *Jesus, Lord and Savior*. Downers Grove: InterVarsity Press, 1986.

Stephen Clark (ed.), *The Forgotten Christ*. Nottingham: Apollos, 2007.

John Calvin, *Institutes of the Christian Religion*, translated F.L. Battles, edited J.T. McNeill, II, xii-xvii, III, i, xxi-xxiv. Philadelphia: Westminster Press, 1960.

Oliver Crisp, *Divinity and Humanity*. Cambridge: Cambridge University Press, 2007.

Oliver Crisp, *God Incarnate*. London: Continuum, 2009.

James Denney, *The Death of Christ*. Repr. Charleston: BiblioBazaar, 2009.

Mark Elliott and John L. McPake (eds.), *The Only Hope – Jesus*. Fearn: Christian Focus Publications, 2002.

Millard J. Erickson, *The Word Became Flesh*. Grand Rapids: Baker Academic, 1996.

Gordon D. Fee, *Pauline Christology*. Grand Rapids: Baker Academic, 2007.

P.T. Forsyth, *The Person and Place of Jesus Christ*. Repr. Charleston: BiblioBazaar, 2009.

Simon J. Gathercole, *Jesus the Pre-existent Son*. Grand Rapids: Eerdmans, 2006.

Colin E. Gunton, *Yesterday and Today: Study of Continuities in Christology*. 2nd edn. London: SPCK, 1997.

Stephen Holmes and Murray Rae (eds.), *The Person of Christ*. London: Continuum, 2005.

C.S. Lewis, *Mere Christianity*. Reissue. London: Collins, 2011.

Richard N. Longenecker (ed.), *Contours of Christology in the New Testament*. Grand Rapids: Eerdmans, 2005.

Douglas McCready, *He Came Down from Heaven*. Downers Grove and Leicester: InterVarsity Press and Apollos, 2005.

J. Gresham Machen, *The Virgin Birth of Christ*. Cambridge: James Clarke and Co., 1958.

Alister E. McGrath, *Incarnation*. London: SPCK, 2005.

BIBLIOGRAPHY

Donald Macleod, *From Glory to Golgotha*. Fearn: Christian Focus Publications, 2002.

Donald Macleod, *Jesus is Lord*. Fearn: Christian Focus Publications, 2005.

Donald Macleod, *The Person of Christ*. Leicester and Downers Grove: Apollos and InterVarsity Press, 1998.

Christopher W. Morgan and Robert A. Peterson, *The Deity of Christ*. Theology in Community. Downers Grove: Crossway Books, 2011.

John Owen, *The Death of Christ*. Repr. Fearn: Christian Focus Publications, 2008.

Robert L. Reymond, *Jesus: Divine Messiah*. Repr. Fearn: Christian Focus Publications, 2003.

Fred Sanders and Klaus Issler, *Jesus in Trinitarian Perspective*. Nashville: Broadman & Holman Publishers, 2007.

Alan Spence, *Christology: a guide for the perplexed*. London: T&T Clark, 2008.

James Stewart, *The Life and Teaching of Jesus Christ*. Repr. Nashville: Abingdon Press, 2000.

Thomas Torrance, *Incarnation*, edited Robert T. Walker. Downers Grove and Milton Keynes: InterVarsity Press and Paternoster, 2008.

Thomas Weinandy, *Does God Suffer?* Edinburgh: T&T Clark, 2000.

Ben Witherington III, *The Christology of Jesus*. Minneapolis: Fortress, 1997.

About the Author

H. Dermot McDonald was born in Ireland in 1911 and became a Christian at a Brethren assembly in Dublin. He became active in open-air preaching and was skilled in discussion of the faith with sometimes hostile audiences. Throughout his career he was renowned for his fluent preaching, his wit and his fondness for debate.

He entered Spurgeon's College in Dublin in 1931, where he lived frugally in order to pay for his theological studies and completed his course despite a long and crippling illness. He was ordained as a Baptist minister, and, after serving as assistant pastor at Harcourt Street in Dublin, he held pastorates in Portrush, Stockton-on-Tees and Woolwich.

In 1948 he became lecturer in Historical Theology and Philosophy of Religion at London Bible College (now the London School of Theology), and he served as Vice-Principal from 1954 and as Acting Principal in 1966. He obtained the degrees of BA Hons,

BD Hons and PhD from the University of London, which also awarded him in 1967 the prestigious Doctor of Divinity degree for outstanding work in the fields of historical theology and philosophy of religion.

Dr McDonald was Special Visiting Professor at various seminaries in the United States, including Northern Baptist Theological Seminary in Chicago, Trinity Evangelical Divinity School in Deerfield, and Winona Lake School of Theology, and also at Regent College in Vancouver, Canada. His numerous books and articles included his doctoral thesis, *Ideas of Revelation*, and its sequel, *Theories of Revelation*, and works on numerous aspects of historical theology.

Dr McDonald was a robust defender of the Christian faith, and was commended for his "uncompromising fidelity to Biblical truth". After his retirement from London Bible College in 1975 he remained active for many years in lecturing and writing. He died in 2001.